LB160
Professional communication skills for business studies

The Open Un

Resource
Book

1

Analysing
Business
Cases

This publication forms part of an Open University course LB160 *Professional communication skills for business studies*. Details of this and other Open University courses can be obtained from the Student Registration and Enquiry Service, The Open University, PO Box 197, Milton Keynes MK7 6BJ, United Kingdom: tel. +44 (0)845 300 60 90, email general-enquiries@open.ac.uk

Alternatively, you may visit the Open University website at http://www.open.ac.uk where you can learn more about the wide range of courses and packs offered at all levels by The Open University.

To purchase a selection of Open University course materials visit http://www.ouw.co.uk, or contact Open University Worldwide, Michael Young Building, Walton Hall, Milton Keynes MK7 6AA, United Kingdom for a brochure. tel. +44 (0)1908 858793; fax +44 (0)1908 858787; email ouw-customer-services@open.ac.uk

The Open University

Walton Hall, Milton Keynes

MK7 6AA

First published 2008. Second edition 2009

Edited and designed by The Open University

Typeset by S&P Enterprises Ltd., Lydbrook, Glos.

Printed in the United Kingdom by Martins the Printers, Berwick-upon-Tweed.

ISBN 978 1 8487 3212 4

2.1

FSC

Mixed Sources

Product group from well-managed forests and other controlled sources

Cert no. TT-COC-2200
www.fsc.org
© 1996 Forest Stewardship Council

Contents

Session 1 resources

Extract 1.1

Last year our Head of Sales retired and I decided to apply for the job.
I had been a Sales Executive for about four years and been pretty
successful. I'd had good appraisals every year, gained three
consecutive merit bonuses, been asked to take on several important
client accounts and helped mentor a new member of staff. So
although I was confident of getting an interview, I was still surprised
when they offered me the job. But that wasn't the only surprise.
When I took up the job three weeks later, it proved very different to
my expectations.

Content		Organisation		Language		Writer		Reader		Purpose	
Person	☐	Story	☐	Formal	☐	Lecturer	☐	Student	☐	Education	☐
Organisation	☐	Description	☐	Informal	☐	Journalist	☐	Public	☐	Entertainment	☐
Industry	☐			Personal	☐					Information	☐
				Impersonal	☐						

Extract 1.2

Handy Snack (Distributing) Co. is a food and drink distribution
company with more than 1500 employees and gross annual sales in
excess of £52 million. The company purchases snack foods (peanuts,
crisps, etc.) as well as bottled and tinned drinks (ranging from fruit
juices to exotic alcoholic cocktail drinks), and distributes them to
independent retailers throughout the UK and Ireland. Competition
in the industry is intense and competitors [like Sunflower
Incorporated] are continually updating product lines in a bid to gain
market share.

Content		Organisation		Language		Writer		Reader		Purpose	
Person	☐	Story	☐	Formal	☐	Lecturer	☐	Student	☐	Education	☐
Organisation	☐	Description	☐	Informal	☐	Journalist	☐	Public	☐	Entertainment	☐
Industry	☐			Personal	☐					Information	☐
				Impersonal	☐						

Extract 1.3

AA set for a float vote

The Automobile Association was inundated yesterday with callers wanting to join as it emerged that the motoring organisation is considering a building society-style demutualisation that could produce windfall payouts of up to £350 for millions of members.

The rush to join the AA came amid speculation that car group Ford might be ready to offer £1.5bn for the organisation. At the same time the AA's Basingstoke head office confirmed that it now has 'an open mind' about its future structure. Less than a year ago the AA insisted 'mutuality is for us'.

Content		Organisation		Language		Writer		Reader		Purpose	
Person	☐	Story	☐	Formal	☐	Lecturer	☐	Student	☐	Education	☐
Organisation	☐	Description	☐	Informal	☐	Journalist	☐	Public	☐	Entertainment	☐
Industry	☐			Personal	☐					Information	☐
				Impersonal	☐						

Extract 1.4

Overall, the US airline industry is in a terrible financial state. Last year alone, operators lost about $8bn on top of the more than $7bn they lost in 2001. The six biggest carriers – American, United, Delta Air Lines, Northwest Airlines, Continental and US Airways – have all suffered badly.

Southwest Airlines was the only significant carrier that did not cut back operations last year and its profitability, amid a sea of losses, has earned it a stock market value bigger than all its rivals combined.

Content		Organisation		Language		Writer		Reader		Purpose	
Person	☐	Story	☐	Formal	☐	Lecturer	☐	Student	☐	Education	☐
Organisation	☐	Description	☐	Informal	☐	Journalist	☐	Public	☐	Entertainment	☐
Industry	☐			Personal	☐					Information	☐
				Impersonal	☐						

Extract 1.5

In the early 1990s, as the first factories in Indonesia were opened, the leading training shoe companies' strategy of using low-cost Asian labour to manufacture their products came under increasing scrutiny from human rights groups, Christian organisations and even academic institutions. By the end of the decade, campaign groups aimed at stamping out this so-called 'sweatshop' production were active in the USA, the UK and Australia. Media interest in the topic was widespread, to the extent that UK magazine *The Big Issue* was urging its readers not to buy Nike trainers and US satirist Garry Trudeau featured the subject in an 11-part *Doonesbury* cartoon series.

Extract 1.6

In the context of the Nike case study, a stakeholder can be defined as any person or group of people who are in some way affected, directly or indirectly, by the activities of Nike. It can also refer to a person or group that can affect the activities of Nike. It is this latter group of stakeholders which will be discussed in this essay.

The Stakeholder Model of the Business Environment is the name given to a model described by Mintzberg as showing a 'cast of players' that occur in and around any organisation (Mintzberg 1983, in Lucas 2000, p. 14). The model provides a diagrammatic view of the different groups that affect and are affected by an organisation. The groups are shown to be in different levels of association with the company; employees being 'close' and government agencies being further away for example. The model provides a list of categories of different groups of individuals and is a framework for the analysis of any organisation. In this example it is used to ascertain the context of the wider environment applicable to the Nike organisation.

The table below lists a number of key groups who influence Nike, as is shown by the case study. The table gives a suggested priority ranking which will be discussed later.

Stakeholder group	Nike example	Where influence comes from	Priority ranking
Owners	Holders of Nike equity share capital	Make up of Nike board. Indirectly affect company share price and thus market capitalisation through buying and selling decisions	B
	Providers of debt finance to Nike	Little influence operationally, except that cost of debt financing can affect company profitability	C
Employees	Nike directors and senior managers	Strategic aspects of the company including product range, sales markets, production methods and locations	A
Publics	Consumers	Purchase Nike products and have influence on product range and product price	A
National governments	Governments within country of ownership (USA)	Influence cost of labour through minimum wage legislation	B

Extract 1.7

Analysing stakeholders

The analysis of stakeholders involves identifying who they are and considering their power and interest with regard to the organisation. Stakeholders can be identified by brainstorming and shown on a stakeholder diagram [...]. Once identified, the relative power and interest of the stakeholders can be mapped onto a power and interest matrix [...]. Additionally this analysis can be extended to consider the reaction, behaviour and position of stakeholders if a particular strategy or plan were to be implemented by the organisation.

Stakeholders with high power and high interest (category D)

Stakeholders with high power and high interest are key players in the organisation and are often involved in managing the organisation and its future.

Content		Organisation		Language		Writer		Reader		Purpose	
Person	☐	Story	☐	Formal	☐	Lecturer	☐	Student	☐	Education	☐
Organisation	☐	Description	☐	Informal	☐	Journalist	☐	Public	☐	Entertainment	☐
Industry	☐	Explanation	☐	Personal	☐	Business person	☐			Information	☐
Assignment	☐	Instruction	☐	Impersonal	☐	Student	☐				

Extract 1.8

The Automobile Association and the question of demutualisation

The Automobile Association (AA) was founded in 1905 by a group of motoring enthusiasts. It was set up as a mutual association. This means that it was owned by its members who had the right to elect the board of directors but did not receive any profits from the organisation. Its founders believed that by joining together as a group of motorists they could obtain better motoring services than they would as individuals. At the time there were many mutual associations owned by their members. The best examples were building societies.

By 1999 the AA had grown into a major organisation. It held around half the motor breakdown market, a market that was experiencing significant change. These changes included the acquisition of Green Flag by Cendant, the entry of the insurance company Direct Line into the market, and the RAC's expected trade sale or flotation.

Content		Organisation		Language		Writer		Reader		Purpose	
Person	☐	Story	☐	Formal	☐	Lecturer	☐	Student	☐	Education	☐
Organisation	☐	Description	☐	Informal	☐	Journalist	☐	Public	☐	Entertainment	☐
Industry	☐	Explanation	☐	Personal	☐	Business person	☐			Information	☐
Assignment	☐	Instruction	☐	Impersonal	☐	Student	☐				

Extract 1.9

Assignment 01 is a case study based on an important event in the history of the Automobile Association of Great Britain. It is marked out of 100 and is worth 10% of the total continuous assessment component.

Part I (90 marks) is intended to:

- assess students' understanding of the key learning points contained within Book 1
- develop skills such as comprehension, presenting information and communicating in writing
- introduce students to the use of short case studies in business studies and develop basic skills of case study analysis.

The case study

Part I of Assignment 01 is based on the following case study of the Automobile Association. [See Extract 1.8.]

The question

Use the stakeholder model of the business environment to analyse the main influences on the AA during its demutualisation process. (50 marks) (maximum 750 words)

Student assignment guidance

This question draws on the stakeholder model which is explained in brief in Chapter 2 of the Reader and on page 13 of the Study Guide (and used to analyse the political environment in Chapter 18, pp. 184–87). In this question you are asked to apply the model to the case material from 'The Automobile Association and the question of demutualisation' to produce an analysis of the external and internal environmental influences on the AA. You may also find it helpful to refer to some of the other models referred to in the remainder of Reader Chapter 2 and Section 2 of the Study Guide in producing your final analysis.

You should write your answer in the form of an essay. Do not forget to reference the course material you have studied.

Content		Organisation		Language		Writer		Reader		Purpose	
Person	☐	Story	☐	Formal	☐	Lecturer	☐	Student	☐	Education	☐
Organisation	☐	Description	☐	Informal	☐	Journalist	☐	Public	☐	Entertainment	☐
Industry	☐	Explanation	☐	Personal	☐	Business person	☐			Information	☐
Assignment	☐	Instruction	☐	Impersonal	☐	Student	☐				

Extract 1.10

100 years of working for road users

It was a great honour to be asked to follow Sir Brian Shaw as Chairman of The AA Motoring Trust (the AA Trust). Sir Brian, who retired at the end of 2005, was Chairman of the AA at the time of its demutualisation and purchase by Centrica plc, and he secured assurances that its historic role as the voice of the motorist would continue. In furtherance of this objective, he was instrumental in establishing the AA Trust in 2002 and guiding its early development. [...]

The Review of the year explains the work undertaken in 2005. It is an impressive body of work, covering a wide spectrum of topical motoring policy issues. Taking on such a broad work programme requires a high level of expertise, experience and commitment. [...]

Content		Organisation		Language		Writer		Reader		Purpose	
Person	☐	Story	☐	Formal	☐	Lecturer	☐	Student	☐	Education	☐
Organisation	☐	Description	☐	Informal	☐	Journalist	☐	Public	☐	Entertainment	☐
Industry	☐	Explanation	☐	Personal	☐	Business person	☐			Information	☐
Assignment	☐	Instruction	☐	Impersonal	☐	Student	☐				

Text 1.11

US airlines: big carriers unlikely to find much relief

Paragraph 1

It has been a difficult year for business travellers in the US. Over the past 12 months US business travellers have been forced to put up with upheaval in airport security systems in the wake of the September 11th (2001) terrorist attacks, the bankruptcy filings of two big airlines, and drastic changes in fares and frequent flyer programmes. The recent bankruptcy filing by UAL, the Chicago-based parent of United Airlines, the world's second largest carrier, is likely to add to the uncertainty.

Paragraph 2

Many are now complaining that airlines, fighting for survival in the midst of one of the industry's worst-ever downturns, are harassing them with measures designed to squeeze additional revenues out of passengers or cut back on perks and benefits. For example, many airlines have tightened up existing cabin baggage regulations and have begun to strictly enforce excess baggage charges – moves designed to acquire additional revenues but which run the risk of alienating many business and other passengers. Several recent newspaper articles have featured passengers who have been charged hundreds of dollars for an extra bag. Business travellers in particular complain that the premium prices they pay for their tickets are not reflected in standards of service.

Paragraph 3

Other airlines have begun to charge an additional fee of up to US$25 if passengers insist on using paper tickets instead of electronic ones. Until they reversed themselves a few weeks ago, many of the big airlines had also begun to charge passengers US$100 if they wanted to fly standby on flights on the same day as their originally scheduled flights. Meanwhile, the bankruptcy filings have left millions wondering whether their frequent-flyer miles are safe. Some airlines including US Air, have already tried to add new restrictions to their frequent-flyer programmes but have been forced to back down in the face of a barrage of criticism from customers.

Paragraph 4

US passengers also face the prospect of fewer scheduled flights and a contraction in routes served by the main 'hub-and-spoke' carriers, including United. In the immediate wake of United's bankruptcy filing, executives said there would be no immediate changes to the company's schedule of 1800 daily flights, providing service to 117 airports around the world. Nevertheless, industry executives and analysts believe United will have to cut back its route system substantially and negotiate further substantial concessions from its employees if it is to survive. They warn that if United manages to restructure and emerge from bankruptcy by June 2004 as planned, it will be a very different airline to the globe-straddling carrier that profited handsomely, selling high-price last-minute tickets to business travellers during the economic boom of the late 1990s.

Paragraph 5

A more immediate concern is that the increasingly likely prospect of a war with Iraq could cause oil prices to spike, further undermining the shaky health of many US airlines and leading to the possibility that other carriers could go bust.

Paragraph 6

But even without an oil price spike, the traditional carriers in the US were already facing fierce competition from cut-price operators such as Southwest Airlines and three-year-old upstart, Jet Blue. Most have acknowledged that they will have to slash costs if they are to survive. The success of low cost 'no-frills' carriers in lucrative markets such as California and the east coast has destroyed the traditional carriers' profits on many routes that they once dominated. For example, Southwest Airlines' share of the California market has jumped to more than 60 per cent in the 18 months while United's share has fallen to less than 20 per cent, in part because losses have forced the big carrier to cut back on its flights. Other low-cost airlines, such as Spirit Airlines and Jet Blue, have begun cutting into the big carriers' business on longer routes.

Paragraph 7

Overall, the US airline industry is in a terrible financial state. Last year alone, operators lost about US$8bn on top of the more than US$7bn they lost in 2001. The six biggest carriers and US Airways – have been forced to cut back operations last year and its profitability, amid a sea of losses, has earned it a stock market value bigger than all its rivals combined.

Paragraph 8

Faced with the success of the low-price carriers and the underlying downturn in passenger traffic, most carriers have been forced to cut their already heavily discounted economy fares further. According to estimates, the average price to fly a mile, adjusted for inflation, fell by 25 per cent in the 10 years to 2001. Since they were unable to raise the prices they charged leisure travellers for fares booked well in advance, most big carriers have raised prices for last minute bookings and business fares. In some cases a business ticket is now almost six times as expensive as a discount ticket.

Paragraph 9

The widening gap between business and discounted economy fares has prompted many companies to re-examine their business travel policies, cancel trips and in some cases abandon the deals they had previously negotiated with big carriers. At the same time, the internet has made it much easier for both business and leisure travellers to compare prices and tinker with itineraries in order to save money.

Paragraph 10

This is not the first time the US airline industry has been plunged into financial turmoil. Since the government deregulated the industry in 1978, it has faced two serious recessions in the early 1980s and 1990s. But the combination of the fear created by September 2001 terrorist attacks, competition from cut-price airlines and the growing sophistication of travellers who now have access to comparative fare information via the internet makes this downturn different, say analysts. With the continuing uncertainty over the US economic recovery and geopolitics, the big carriers are unlikely to find much relief this year. For business travellers, that may translate into further uncertainty and turmoil.

(Source: adapted from Taylor, P., 2003, 'US airlines: big carriers unlikely to find much relief', *Financial Times*, 30 January)

Extract 1.12

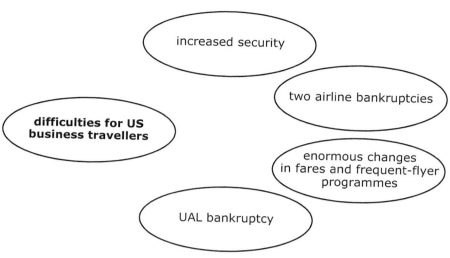

Figure 1.1   Mind map for Extract 1.12

[1] It has been a difficult year for business travellers in the US. [2] There has been inconvenience for them, first, because of the increased security at airports after the terrorist attacks in September 2001. [3] Second, two big airline companies have filed for bankruptcy. [4] Third, there have been enormous changes in the prices that they pay for fares and in the special offers they get for flying frequently with the same airline. [5] Finally, there is going to be more uncertainty because UAL, which is the parent company for United Airlines, has recently filed for bankruptcy.

Extract 1.13

Figure 1.2   Mind map for Extract 1.13

[1] Many business travellers are now complaining that the airline companies are causing difficulties for travellers by trying to get more income from them or by not giving them free gifts and benefits. [2] The airline companies are doing this because they are fighting to survive in a very bad period for the airline industry. [3] For example, many airline companies have increased the regulations on cabin baggage and they are making sure that they always charge passengers for bringing too much baggage on the plane. [4] The airlines are doing this in order to increase their income. [5] However, the actions are likely to make passengers angry with these companies and try to find alternative ways to travel. [6] Recently, there have been several newspaper articles reporting passengers who have been charged hundreds of dollars for an extra bag. [7] Business travellers in particular are complaining that they do not receive a very good service for the extremely high price they pay for their tickets.

Extract 1.14

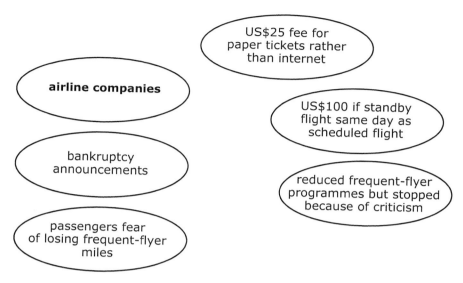

Figure 1.3 Mind map for Extract 1.14

[1] Other airlines have begun to charge an extra fee of up to $25 if passengers want to use paper tickets instead of buying tickets through the internet. [2] Until they changed their minds a few weeks ago, many of the big airlines were charging passengers $100 if they were not able to get onto their scheduled flight but still wanted to go on a standby flight on the same day. [3] At the same time, millions of passengers are wondering whether they will lose their frequent-flyer miles because of the bankruptcy announcements by the airlines. [4] Some airlines, including US Air, have tried to reduce what they offer on their frequent-flyer programmes but they had to stop that because there was so much criticism from customers.

Extract 1.15

Case study text	Notes
It has been a difficult year for business travellers in the US.	difficult year for business travellers = business has been bad in the USA
Over the past 12 months US business travellers have been forced to put up with upheaval in airport security systems in the wake of the September 11th (2001) terrorist attacks, the bankruptcy filings of two big airlines, and drastic changes in fares and frequent-flyer programmes.	forced to put up with = had to accept airport security systems = locks on airport doors in the wake of = because of bankruptcy filings = official registration by company that it has no money drastic = unwelcome how many difficulties? = four
The recent bankruptcy filing by UAL, the Chicago-based parent of United Airlines, the world's second largest carrier, is likely to add to the uncertainty.	Chicago-based parent = person who lives in Chicago is likely to add to the uncertainty = uncertain whether the situation will get worse
Many are now complaining that airlines, fighting for survival in the midst of one of the industry's worst-ever downturns, are harassing them with measures designed to squeeze additional revenues out of passengers or cut back on perks and benefits.	Many = many airlines fighting for survival = passengers fighting for survival one of the industry's worst-ever downturns = airline industry's worsening performance are harassing them = passengers complaining about airlines measures designed to squeeze additional revenues out of passengers = actions intended to get more money from passengers
For example, many airlines have tightened up existing cabin baggage regulations and have begun to strictly enforce excess baggage charges – moves designed to acquire additional revenues but which run the risk of alienating many business and other passengers.	tightened up = made stricter existing regulations = out-of-date regulations strictly enforce = made stricter excess baggage = extra baggage moves = actions acquire additional revenues = obtain extra income run the risk of alienating passengers = might send passengers overseas
Several recent newspaper articles have featured passengers who have been charged hundreds of dollars for an extra bag.	featured = focused on charged hundreds of dollars = asked to pay hundreds of dollars
Business travellers in particular complain that the premium prices they pay for their tickets are not reflected in standards of service.	premium prices = top prices not reflected in standards of service = services are not top quality
Other airlines have begun to charge an additional fee of up to US$25 if passengers insist on using paper tickets instead of electronic ones.	charge an additional fee = passengers pay more for electronic tickets than paper ones

Until they reversed themselves a few weeks ago, many of the big airlines had also begun to charge passengers US$100 if they wanted to fly standby on flights on the same day as their originally scheduled flights.	they reversed themselves a few weeks ago = they introduced the charge a few weeks ago
	fly standby = fly in an alternative, substitute plane
	scheduled flight = cancelled flight = it is more expensive to fly standby on the same day as the original scheduled flight
Meanwhile, the bankruptcy filings have left millions wondering whether their frequent-flyer miles are safe.	wondering whether their frequent flyer miles are safe = passengers are worried about airline safety
Some airlines, including US Air, have already tried to add new restrictions to their frequent-flyer programmes but have been forced to back down in the face of a barrage of criticism from customers.	restrictions to frequent-flyer programmes = limitations to the special services they offer to passengers who use planes frequently
	forced to back down in the face of a barrage of criticism from customers = made to change their minds by the strong objections from passengers

(Source: adapted from Taylor, P., 2003, 'US airlines: big carriers unlikely to find much relief', *Financial Times*, 30 January)

Extract 1.16

US airlines: big carriers unlikely to find much relief

(P = paragraph.)

[P4] US passengers also face the prospect of fewer scheduled flights and a contraction in routes served by the main 'hub-and-spoke' carriers, including United.

[P5] A more immediate concern is that the increasingly likely prospect of a war with Iraq could cause oil prices to spike, further undermining the shaky health of many US airlines and leading to the possibility that other carriers could go bust.

[P6] But even without an oil price spike, the traditional carriers in the US were already facing fierce competition from cut-price operators such as Southwest Airlines and three-year-old upstart, Jet Blue.

[P7] Overall, the US airline industry is in a terrible financial state. Last year alone, operators lost about US$8bn on top of the more than US$7bn they lost in 2001.

[P8] Faced with the success of the low-price carriers and the underlying downturn in passenger traffic, most carriers have been forced to cut their already heavily discounted economy fares further.

[P9] The widening gap between business and discounted economy fares has prompted many companies to re-examine their business travel policies, cancel trips and, in some cases, abandon the deals they had previously negotiated with big carriers.

[P10 beginning] This is not the first time the US airline industry has been plunged into financial turmoil.

[P10 end] With the continuing uncertainty over the US economic recovery and geopolitics, the big carriers are unlikely to find much relief this year. For business travellers, that may translate into further uncertainty and turmoil.

(Source: adapted from Taylor, 2003, op. cit.)

Text 1.17

Original case study text	Notes
Paragraph 1 It has been a difficult year for business travellers in the US. Over the past 12 months US business travellers have been forced to put up with upheaval in airport security systems in the wake of the September 11th (2001) terrorist attacks, the bankruptcy filings of two big airlines, and drastic changes in fares and frequent flyer programmes. The recent bankruptcy filing by UAL, the Chicago-based parent of United Airlines, the world's second largest carrier, is likely to add to the uncertainty.	[P1] disturbances for business travellers terrorist-induced upheaval in airport security two airline bankruptcies drastic changes in fares and frequent-flyer programmes UAL bankruptcy
Paragraph 2 Many are now complaining that airlines, fighting for survival in the midst of one of the industry's worst-ever downturns, are harassing them with measures designed to squeeze additional revenues out of passengers or cut back on perks and benefits. For example, many airlines have tightened up existing cabin baggage regulations and have begun to strictly enforce excess baggage charges – moves designed to acquire additional revenues but which run the risk of alienating many business and other passengers. Several recent newspaper articles have featured passengers who have been charged hundreds of dollars for an extra bag. Business travellers in particular complain that the premium prices they pay for their tickets are not reflected in standards of service.	[P2] complaints about airline harassment/ industry's worst ever downturn
Paragraph 3 Other airlines have begun to charge an additional fee of up to US$25 if passengers insist on using paper tickets instead of electronic ones. Until they reversed themselves a few weeks ago, many of the big airlines had also begun to charge passengers US$100 if they wanted to fly standby on flights on the same day as their originally scheduled flights. Meanwhile, the bankruptcy filings have left millions wondering whether their frequent-flyer miles are safe. Some airlines including US Air, have already tried to add new restrictions to their frequent-flyer programmes but have been forced to back down in the face of a barrage of criticism from customers.	[P3] charge for paper tickets

Paragraph 4

US passengers also face <u>the prospect of fewer scheduled flights and a contraction in routes served by the main 'hub-and-spoke' carriers, including United</u>. In the immediate wake of United's bankruptcy filing, executives said there would be no immediate changes to the company's schedule of 1800 daily flights, providing service to 117 airports around the world. Nevertheless, industry executives and analysts believe United will have to cut back its route system substantially and negotiate further substantial concessions from its employees if it is to survive. They warn that if United manages to restructure and emerge from bankruptcy by June 2004 as planned, it will be a very different airline to the globe-straddling carrier that profited handsomely, selling high-price last-minute tickets to business travellers during the economic boom of the late 1990s.

[P4] likelihood of reduced number of scheduled flights and routes

Paragraph 5

<u>A more immediate concern is that the increasingly likely prospect of a war with Iraq could cause oil prices to spike, further undermining the shaky health of many US airlines and leading to the possibility that other carriers could go bust.</u>

[P5] prospects of war with Iraq → oil price rise and more bankruptcies

Paragraph 6

But even without an oil price spike, <u>the traditional carriers in the US were already facing fierce competition from cut-price operators</u> such as Southwest Airlines and three-year-old upstart, Jet Blue. <u>Most have acknowledged that they will have to slash costs if they are to survive.</u> The success of low cost 'no-frills' carriers in lucrative markets such as California and the east coast has destroyed the traditional carriers' profits on many routes that they once dominated. For example, Southwest Airlines' share of the California market has jumped to more than 60 per cent in the 18 months while United's share has fallen to less than 20 per cent, in part because losses have forced the big carrier to cut back on its flights. Other low-cost airlines, such as Spirit Airlines and Jet Blue, have begun cutting into the big carriers' business on longer routes.

[P6] competition to big carriers from cut-price operators

Paragraph 7

Overall, the US airline industry is in a terrible financial state. Last year alone, operators lost about US$8bn on top of the more than US$7bn they lost in 2001. The six biggest carriers and US Airways – have been forced to cut back operations last year and its profitability, amid a sea of losses, has earned it a stock market value bigger than all its rivals combined.

[P7] terrible state of airline industry

Paragraph 8

Faced with the success of the low-price carriers and the underlying downturn in passenger traffic, most carriers have been forced to cut their already heavily discounted economy fares further. According to estimates, the average price to fly a mile, adjusted for inflation, fell by 25 per cent in the 10 years to 2001. Since they were unable to raise the prices they charged leisure travellers for fares booked well in advance, most big carriers have raised prices for last minute bookings and business fares. In some cases a business ticket is now almost six times as expensive as a discount ticket.

[P8] cuts in economy fares

Paragraph 9

The widening gap between business and discounted economy fares has prompted many companies to re-examine their business travel policies, cancel trips and in some cases abandon the deals they had previously negotiated with big carriers. At the same time, the internet has made it much easier for both business and leisure travellers to compare prices and tinker with itineraries in order to save money.

[P9] companies cancelling contracts with big carriers

Paragraph 10

This is not the first time the US airline industry has been plunged into financial turmoil. Since the government deregulated the industry in 1978, it has faced two serious recessions in the early 1980s and 1990s. But the combination of the fear created by September 2001 terrorist attacks, competition from cut-price airlines and the growing sophistication of travellers who now have access to comparative fare information via the internet makes this downturn different, say analysts. With the continuing uncertainty over the US economic recovery and geopolitics, the big carriers are unlikely to find much relief this year. For business travellers, that may translate into further uncertainty and turmoil.

[P10] not first airline crisis
poor prospects for big carriers and business travellers

(Source: adapted from Taylor, P., 2003, 'US airlines: big carriers unlikely to find much relief', *Financial Times*, 30 January)

Text 1.18

AA set for a float vote

The Automobile Association was inundated yesterday with callers wanting to join as it emerged that the motoring organisation is considering a building society-style demutualisation that could produce windfall payouts of up to £350 for millions of members.

The rush to join the AA came amid speculation that car group Ford might be ready to offer £1.5bn for the organisation. At the same time the AA's Basingstoke head office confirmed that it now has 'an open mind' about its future structure. Less than a year ago the AA insisted 'mutuality is for us'.

The AA has also retained one of the City's leading spin-doctors and the investment bank, Schroders, as adviser.

Ford refused to comment yesterday, but the car group has made it clear that it is keen to diversify into motoring services. Last week it paid £1bn for the Kwik-Fit tyre and exhaust business.

In a statement, the road rescue organisation said: 'The AA has always kept an open mind about its structure as it pursues its prime purpose: to serve the best interests of its members. No decisions have yet been made in this respect.' But the AA's management committee, led by chairman Sir Brian Shaw and Director General John Maxwell, is expected to decide by the autumn whether to pursue a change of strategy, abandoning the mutual ownership structure set up when it was founded, in 1905.

Apart from the possibility of a straightforward sell-off the committee is also understood to be considering joint ventures, partnership proposals or a stock market flotation.

A source close to the organisation said: 'They are not ruling anything out. They have got all sorts of strategic possibilities and they are reviewing their options.'

Should the committee decide to demutualise it will have to conduct a poll of its members. The organisation has 9.5 million, but only the 4.3 million full voting members would qualify for a windfall payout. They pay a minimum £43 a year in subscriptions.

The remainder are associate members and would not receive any payouts. They include 1.7 million spouses and children of full members and 3.5 million who can call on the AA for breakdown assistance through a manufacturer's or fleet scheme.

But anyone joining the AA now to cash in on any sell-off could be disappointed. The organisation is free to set a cut-off date prior to yesterday's statement for those members who would qualify.

The AA's decision to reconsider its future ownership comes in the wake of last year's decision to demutualise by the organisation's main rival, the Royal Automobile Club. The RAC agreed a £450m sale of its motoring services business to the American group, Cendant, which promised a payout of some £35,000 a head to its elite 12,000 full members — but the deal was blocked by the government.

Cendant, which already owned the Green Flag breakdown service, has now put that up for sale, and the RAC is simultaneously seeking an alternative buyer and preparing for a flotation in order to unlock the value of the organisation for its members' benefit.

The RAC is expected to provide a progress report some time within the coming fortnight, when the first flotation details will have to be published if the organisation is to achieve its deadline of an early summer listing.

'It is understandable, following the dramatic changes in the breakdown assistance market in the last year, that speculation (about demutualisation) should arise,' said a spokesman from the AA.

(Source: Finch, J., 1999, 'AA set for a float vote', *The Guardian*, 21 April)

Session 2 resources

Extract 2.1

The term 'environment' in this case refers to much more than the ecological, 'green' issues that the word commonly evokes. 'Environment' here is more appropriately interpreted as the external context in which organisations find themselves undertaking their activities. Each organisation has a unique external environment that has unique impacts on the organisation, due to the fact that organisations are located in different places and are involved in different business activities, with different products, services, customers, and so on.

(Source: Capon, C., 2004, *Understanding Organisational Context*, Prentice Hall, p. 278)

Extract 2.2

In recent years, the term 'the environment' has taken on a rather specialised meaning: it involves 'green' issues and the poisoning of our planet by human activity. These concerns are certainly part of our considerations in this book, but we use the term 'the environment' in a much broader sense to describe everything and everyone outside the organisation. This includes customers, competitors, suppliers, distributors, government and social institutions.

(Source: Lynch, R., 2003, *Corporate Strategy*, Pearson Education, Harlow, p. 84)

Extract 2.3

A host of external factors influence a firm's choice of direction and action and, ultimately, its organizational structure and internal processes. These factors which constitute the *external environment*, can be divided into three interrelated subcategories: factors in the *remote* environment, factors in the *industry* environment, and factors in the *operating* environment. (Many authors refer to the operating environment as the *task* or *competitive* environment.) This chapter describes the complex necessities involved in formulating strategies that optimize a firm's market opportunities. Figure 3-1 [not included] suggests the interrelationship between the firm and its remote, its industry, and its operating environments. In combination, these factors form the basis of the opportunities and threats that a firm faces in its competitive environment.

(Source: Pearce, J.A. and Robinson, R. B., 2000, *Strategic Management: formulation, implementation and control*, Irwin McGraw-Hill, p. 71)

Extract 2.4

In Chapter 1, the interdependence between a business organisation and the environment within which it operates was briefly discussed. It was pointed out that society depends on business organisations for most of the products and services it needs, including the employment opportunities which businesses create. Conversely, business organisations depend on society for the resources they need. Business organisations are not self-sufficient, nor are they self-contained. They obtain resources from and are dependent upon the environment in which they operate. Business organisations and society, or, more specifically, the environment in which they function, therefore, depend on each other. This mutual dependence entails a complex relationship between the two. This relationship increases in complexity when certain variables in the environment, such as technological innovation, economic events or political developments, bring about change in the environment which impacts in different ways on the business organisation.

(Source: de J. Cronje, G.J., du Toit, G.S. and Motlatla, M.D.C., eds, 2004, *Introduction to Business Management*, 6th edn, OUP, Oxford pp. 81–2)

Extract 2.5

Every business is engaged in at least one conversion process, converting inputs to outputs. While doing this it is operating in an environment consisting of a great many elements. The elements in the external environment can be classified by the level of influence that they have on the business and the business has on them. As a result a business can be considered to have two environments, depending on the direction of the influences between the business and the elements within them. First there is the *operating environment*, composed of elements that the organisation can influence and that also influence the business. Second there is the *remote environment*, composed of elements on which the individual business has no significant influence but which may have a major effect on the operating environment and on the business.

(Source: Finlay, P., 2000, *Strategic Management*, Pearson Education, Harlow, p. 163)

Extract 2.6

Before introducing the models, I will define the [term] 'Business environment' ... A 'business environment' is a set of external conditions in which an organisation exists and operates. There are two levels of business environment; the market / 'near environment' linked to behaviour of organisations within markets and their competitiveness and the 'wider environment' which are broader trends and controls outside the immediate control of individual organisations which can also shape the way they behave.

(Source: OU Business School student assignment)

Extract 2.7

Business does not operate in a vacuum. There is always an environment, 'a set of external conditions under which a business organisation exists and operates' (Lucas, 2000, p.5). When considering a business, its environment, and the way in which they influence each other, it is useful to have a 'model', which is a simplified picture of the context in which events are taking place. A model helps to identify external influences on a business and analyse their effects on the behaviour of the business.

(Source: OU Business School student assignment)

Extract 2.8

Organisations operate in a market environment, which is their near or immediate environment. However, there are a wider set of environments, which they operate in. These can be explained using the STEP model. There are four environments: Social, Technological, Economic and Political that influence organisations. Whilst organisations usually have control over the near environment it is the wider environment that controls the organisations, although some businesses can influence their wider environment.

(Source: OU Business School student assignment)

Text 2.9

STEP framework

External environments can be defined and analysed using STEP analysis, which examines the categories into which external influences on the organisation can be placed.

- _____ influences on organisations include ... the rules and regulations imposed by government, as well as the influences on organisations of various trade associations, trade unions and chambers of commerce.

- _____ influences on organisations include the impact of banks, stock markets, the world money markets, and trading blocs such as the European Union.

- _____ influences on organisations include changes in the age and structure of populations, the manner in which populations behave, and the way in which the culture of a population or country changes and develops.

- _____ influences include the development of increasingly sophisticated computer hardware and software. The development of media and communications technology covers electronics and telecommunications, including use of the internet. The ongoing development of the internet as a way of doing business and accessing information has meant a whole new 'media' which needs to be understood in terms of its potential use and reliability.

Basic analysis of an organisation's external environment can be done by breaking down the external influences on the organisation into the STEP categories and assessing the impact of the individual elements identified in each category.

(Source: adapted from Capon, C., 2004, *Understanding Organisational Context*, Prentice Hall, p. 279)

Extract 2.10

1   Trainer companies have had to acknowledge that, despite the global status of their products, consumers in different countries have different spending power; therefore, they must tailor their product range and pricing strategy accordingly.

2   Despite their insistence that their products are primarily sports footwear, they have to respond to fashion trends as well, if they want to ensure that a shoe is a commercial success.

3   While Nike, Adidas and Reebok all aim for athletic credibility, the design of their shoes must incorporate the influences and styles of popular culture.

4   They are also able to profit from beneficial trade and tariff agreements, wherever they exist.

5   The 'messages' they use to communicate with various groups of consumers need to be tailored to suit the different market 'sectors' for which they manufacture shoes, while maintaining the integrity of their brand identity.

6   Sales of full-price trainers have also been threatened by supermarket chains importing goods from unauthorised suppliers and selling them at a big discount.

7   Young people are most likely to spend the highest amount, with 28 per cent of 15 to 19 year olds and 27 per cent of 20 to 24 year olds spending over £100 a year on these products.

8   Trainer manufacturers have also responded to the growth in e-commerce – sales of training shoes via the internet. Nike sells shoes via its own website, Nike.com, and also owns internet shoe retailer FogDog.

9   Grant aid was drastically reduced with the result that local authorities either dropped or greatly reduced their insulation programmes.

10   Although the USA was considered by many to be at least 18 months ahead of the rest of the world in exploiting the internet, Europe had a substantial lead in mobile telephony.

11   The US could also move directly to third-generation technology, enabling it to catch up with Europe within the next three to four years, emphasising the need for Europe to prove as effective in third-generation mobile telephony as in the current generation.

12 By the year 2003, communications devices, from computers and televisions to mobile phones, were expected to converge, enabling all to offer the same host of services.

13 For example in 2000, in the UK alone, Vodafone would have to pay £6 billion to the government for their new 20-year licence, on top of an estimated £4 billion of network spending and handset subsidies.

14 It was clear to many observers that by hiving off its attractive telecoms activities into a separate company Mannesmann risked becoming vulnerable to an unwelcome take-over.

15 Tony Blair, the British Prime Minister, however, demanded that Germany treat a British attempt to take over one of its firms with the same fairness extended to Germans buying up businesses in Britain. He rebuked Gerhard Schroeder for fighting the take-over, making it clear that in the new global economy he should not try to block it.

16 There seems to be widespread suspicion in Germany of everything connected with stock markets. Germany does not have a stock exchange culture, as its economy is dominated by medium-sized companies and companies which are not quoted on the stock market.

(Sources: extracts 1–8 from Sturges, J., 2000, 'Keep on running: the training shoe business', B200 case study, OU Business School, Milton Keynes; extract 9 from Wilson, D. and Rosenfeld, H., 1990, *Managing Organisations, Text, Readings and Cases*, McGraw-Hill, p. 357; extracts 10–16 from a case study on Vodafone's takeover of Mannesmann, author unknown, 2000, B200 TMA 07, OU Business School, Milton Keynes)

Extract 2.11

Nike and the vexed issue of corporate responsibility

In the early 1990s, as the first factories in Indonesia were opened, the leading training shoe companies' strategy of using low-cost Asian labour to manufacture their products came under increasing scrutiny from human rights groups, Christian organisations and even academic institutions. By the end of the decade, campaign groups aimed at stamping out this so-called 'sweatshop' production were active in the USA, the UK and Australia. Media interest in the topic was widespread, to the extent that UK magazine *The Big Issue* was urging its readers not to buy Nike trainers and US satirist Garry Trudeau featured the subject in an 11-part *Doonesbury* cartoon series.

Most criticism was aimed at the major trainer manufacturers, especially Nike, for reasons of their size and market dominance. The emphasis Nike and its competitors placed on social betterment through physical fitness in their advertising also made them more vulnerable to accusations of mistreatment of their Asian workers.

Initially, the trainer companies tried to divert criticism by claiming that the issue was the responsibility of their subcontractors, but were soon forced to respond when the subject was drawn to the attention of the US State Department. Eventually they were obliged to draw up codes of conduct in an attempt to eradicate human rights abuses in their factories, raise wages, ban harmful chemicals and eradicate the use of under-age labour. This was not sufficient for their critics; instead, it proved to be the first stage in a cycle of criticism and reaction which is still continuing, with the focus shifting from Indonesia to China and Vietnam, and manufacturers still struggling to establish a socially 'responsible' image.

While criticism of human rights abuses in training shoe factories is clearly justified, it is interesting to examine the trainer manufacturers' operations in the context of the prevailing economic situation in countries such as Vietnam and China. Their presence in these countries can be economically critical. China is now the biggest shoe-producing country in the world; Nike is Vietnam's biggest employer. Jobs are scarce and people want to work for companies like Nike and Reebok. Factory jobs, while badly paid by Western standards, pay twice as much as teachers earn in Vietnam.

Nevertheless, as a result of the continued criticism, corporate responsibility is now a major concern for all trainer companies whose shoes are manufactured in Southeast Asia and China. For example, in 1998 Nike appointed its first new vice-president for corporate and social responsibility and introduced six new corporate responsibility initiatives.

(Source: adapted from Sturges, J., 2000, 'Keep on running: the training shoe business', B200 OU Business School case study, The Open University, pp. 24, 26)

Text 2.12

The growth of closed-circuit television systems

Since 2001, there has been a significant increase in the use of closed-circuit television (CCTV) cameras in public places in the USA and other developed countries. Such cameras have been used in commercial premises in the USA since the early 1970s but, after the terrorist attacks of 11 September 2001, the use of such cameras increased in public areas such as parks and streets. Citizens can now be observed going about their daily business. The number of CCTV cameras in British town centres has rapidly increased in recent years. There are similar increases in Europe and North America. During the early 1990s the total value of the equipment market for CCTV products in the UK was around £100m annually. This rose to £361m between 1996 and 2000.

According to one industry source, 'Double-digit growth in the video surveillance market has created a huge opportunity for software and chip companies to manage these enormous video streams'. International terrorism and homeland security investments are creating an unprecedented 'intelligent video' (IV) growth opportunity with technology playing a major role in future development. New IV networks, automatic edge detection, event characterisation, detailed analytics, and first responder controls represent the future of IV systems just starting to come on line. IV technology represents a major growth opportunity for hardware and software companies wanting to position themselves for growth in the rapidly expanding international security industry. Middle East violence, threats to oil supplies, Chinese and Indian economic growth, Islamic and western cultural tensions, and normal concern for domestic crime will fuel massive potential demand for IV products for a long time to come.

Despite this increasing intrusion into people's personal lives, there seems to be little chance of privacy protections limiting the use of such technologies. In the USA, public area surveillance does not count as a 'search'. The outcome of court cases suggests that even covert CCTV surveillance in public areas is lawful.

Civil libertarians and law reform groups have raised concerns about the current lack of statutory controls over the use of public space CCTV. In China, advanced traffic control systems were used to identify thousands of people involved in the Tiananmen Square protests of 1989. In the UK, although the technology behind CCTV has been available since the 1970s, its adoption has been slowed down by political concerns. For example, although the police are keen to have systems adopted, socialist-leaning local authorities have been less welcoming. This was particularly because research showed that the technology could be used against trade unionists, peace campaigners and animal-rights activists. Financial constraints on the spending powers of local authorities also played a role in slowing down the adoption of CCTV technology.

Nevertheless, in the UK, the impetus for the adoption of the technology came with increasing levels of crime in the 1980s and the adoption of privatisation of various public services. This effectively reduced the immediate cost to the public purse of adopting the technology. Also aiding the adoption of the technology was a specific event, the murder of a child in Merseyside. His abduction, which was widely covered in the popular press, was caught on CCTV and this led to the capture of his assailants. As a result, CCTV became more acceptable.

In the UK, CCTV is also being widely used in the field of transport. According to a commentator, 'many cities, such as Bangkok or Buenos Aires, will accept relatively high levels of congestion, but paralysing gridlock just isn't economically, socially or politically acceptable in London'. So each part of London's transport network, buses, underground system and roads – have separate central operations rooms, operating 24 hours a day, seven days a week.

In the medical arena, as well, the CCTV revolution is becoming more prevalent. According to a small-scale evaluation project, residents in a medium secure unit generally supported the use of CCTV at night because it made them feel safer. For example, some respondents said CCTV recordings helped to cut the risk of their property being stolen, while the fire risk was lessened because patients were less likely to smoke in their rooms. It was also popular with patients who disliked being woken up during traditional night-time checks.

Larger evaluation studies have shown more mixed results. In the UK, where reviews have been more common and comprehensive, findings about the effects on crime have been mixed. One recent study compared 13 evaluations of CCTV in city centres and public housing. Of these, five found positive effects (a reduction in offences), three reported undesirable outcomes (actual increases in crime), while in the remaining five studies there appeared to be no effect or the results were unclear.

Mixed findings such as these seem difficult to reconcile with the enthusiasm for public CCTV among local and state governments in Australia. Crime reduction is only one of the rationales for installing a camera system. Another is a desire to improve public perceptions of safety, where Australian evidence is more positive. Research in New South Wales among members of the public reported that the presence of the cameras made them feel safer in the central business district. However, a study for the City of Melbourne found that its cameras had not affected public perceptions.

Concerns about public perceptions help explain the economic and political forces pushing many jurisdictions into installing CCTV systems. They link the uptake of public space CCTV to social trends such as the rise of the 'stranger society'. In contemporary post-industrial contexts, people tend to become more remote from familial and other traditional constraints, and to become dislocated from community networks. Hence a perceived desire for techniques and procedures, which provide reassurance that public behaviour is being monitored.

Global economic trends also increase pressures on town and city centres to attract their share of tourists, other consumers and investors. CCTV can play an important role in marketing an urban centre as relatively safe. However, it can also exacerbate tendencies to exclude homeless, unemployed and other marginalised people whose presence detracts from the 'positive vision' that image makers try to convey.

References

McCahill, M. and Norris, C. (2002) 'CCTV in Britain', *Working Paper No. 3*, March, Centre for Criminology and Criminal Justice, University of Hull.

Mental Health Practice (2006) 'Patients positive about CCTV', September, Vol. 10, No. 1.

Murray, L. (2006) 'Keeping London moving', *Geographical*, May [online], www.geographical.co.uk

www.jpfreeman.com/mktreport.htm#report7

www.indigovision.com/site/sections/investor/pdf/Full%20Annual%20Report%202006.pdf

uninews.unimelb.edu.au/articleid_760.html

Example STEP analysis – notes on the growth of CCTV systems

Social:

- increased social acceptance of CCTV
- increases in crime and terrorism
- people's perception that CCTV can make their lives safer
- high profile cases where CCTV used to catch criminals
- public opinion that the benefits of such systems outweigh the costs
- growth of the 'stranger society'
- people have fewer links to their social environment
- feelings of security.

Technological:

- increasingly more versatile or greater functionality
- intelligent video and internet protocol
- cheaper products due to technological developments.

Economic:

- CCTV cameras more affordable due to economic growth
- private sector financing in public sector expenditure so sales not always involving large government expense
- equipment leased from private sector firms making it more affordable
- wider political acceptance of private sector funding for public projects
- local governments need to encourage investment and promote tourism and people's feeling of security
- CCTV keeps existing residents or businesses happy, and encourages new ones
- CCTV for traffic management to reduce congestion.

Political:

- more (political) acceptance of CCTV
- increasing crime and terrorism
- despite concerns about personal liberty and human rights
- US law allows use of CCTV; not a 'search'; covert use in public places
- fairly liberal political or legal environment towards CCTV
- no statutory controls over the use of public space CCTV.

(Source: Haider Ali, 2007, Open University Business School, Milton Keynes)

Text 2.13

Analysing stakeholders

The analysis of stakeholders involves identifying who they are and considering their power and interest with regard to the organisation. Stakeholders can be identified by brainstorming and shown on a stakeholder diagram. Once identified, the relative power and interest of the stakeholders can be mapped onto a power and interest matrix [diagram]. Additionally this analysis can be extended to consider the reaction, behaviour and position of stakeholders if a particular strategy or plan were to be implemented by the organisation.

Stakeholders with high power and high interest (category D)

Stakeholders with high power and high interest are key players in the organisation and are often involved in managing the organisation and its future. If key players are not directly involved in managing the organisation, it is vital that they are given serious consideration in the development of long-term plans and the future direction of the organisation, as they have the power to block proposed plans and implement their own alternative agenda.

Stakeholders with high power and low interest (category C)

Stakeholders with high power and low interest are those who must be kept satisfied, for example institutional shareholders. Institutional shareholders will often remain compliant while they receive acceptable returns on their investment and are pleased with the organisation's management and activities. However, the ability of category C stakeholders to reposition themselves on the power and interest matrix into category D and become stakeholders with a continuing high degree of power and an increase in their level of interest should not be under-estimated. [...]

Stakeholders with low power and high interest (category B)

The stakeholders in category B are those with low power and high interest, who are able to exert relatively little power in influencing the organisation and its actions. However, these stakeholders have a high level of interest in the organisation and will voice their concerns if that interest is not being considered in a suitable manner. [...]

Stakeholders with low power and low interest (category A)

Stakeholders with low power and low interest are those in whom the organisation need invest only minimal effort. However, category A stakeholders should not be ignored as they may acquire a stake in the organisation by becoming, for example, a customer, supplier or competitor, which will mean an increased level of interest and/or power.

(Source: Capon, C., 2004, *Understanding Organisational Context*, Prentice Hall, pp. 387–8, 389)

Text 2.14

The Automobile Association and the question of demutualisation

The Automobile Association was founded in 1905 by a group of motoring enthusiasts. It was set up as a mutual association. This means that it was owned by its members who had the right to elect the board of directors but did not receive any profits from the organisation. Its founders believed that by joining together as a group of motorists they could obtain better motoring services than they would as individuals. At the time there were many mutual associations owned by their members. The best examples were building societies.

By 1999 the AA had grown into a major organisation. It held around half the motor breakdown market, a market that was experiencing significant change. These changes included the acquisition of Green Flag by Cendant, the entry of the insurance company Direct Line into the market, and the RAC's expected trade sale or flotation.

During the 1990s, many mutual associations had 'demutualised'. That is they changed from being mutual associations with members to being public limited companies with shareholders. These shareholders could now receive a share of the profits of the organisation. When an organisation demutualised, the members of the organisation also received a windfall payment which was often very large. For this reason demutualisation was usually very popular with members of mutual associations.

In April 1999 the AA began to consider its options with regard to retaining its mutual status or demutualising. It was rumoured that Ford had informally approached the AA with a takeover offer that would end the latter's mutual status. Other interested bidders were thought to include Centrica and a number of venture capitalists. The then Director-General of the AA, John Maxwell, initiated a strategic review to allow the AA to assess its options. The options available included demutualisation, a joint venture with a suitable partner or takeover by another company. The merchant bank Schroders was advising the AA.

In 1999 the AA had annual sales of around £600 million from its businesses, which included roadside service, publications and driving schools, and its value was estimated to between £1 billion and £1.5 billion. Pursuit of the demutualisation option and stock-market flotation would give each full member of the AA a moderate windfall of £200–250. In 1999 the AA had 9.5 million members, of which 4.3 million were full-paying members who would receive the windfall payouts. However, excluded from the demutualisation windfall were the 1.7 million associate members, including the families of full-paying members who benefit from the association's services, and the 3.5 million members who are drivers of fleet cars with AA cover and drivers who received their AA membership as part of a package when purchasing a car.

The members of the AA were balloted in August 1999 on the proposed sale of the AA to Centrica. The result of the ballot was announced in mid-September 1999 and showed 67 per cent of eligible members voted and 96 per cent of them voted in favour of the sale. The sale to Centrica was completed in July 2000 for £1.1 billion.

(Source: adapted from Capon, C., 2004, *Understanding Organisational Context*, Prentice Hall, pp. 389–90)

Extract 2.15

Use the stakeholder model of the business environment to analyse the main influences on the Automobile Association during its demutualisation process.

Heading _____

The category _____stakeholders are those with _____power and _____ interest. For the AA, non-members fell into this category. They were unable to receive breakdown services from the organisation and had _____ influence over its demutualisation decision. However, it should be recognised that stakeholders' power and influence can alter over time. The opportunity of a £200–250 windfall might have encouraged some non-members to become members and move to category _____, _____ interest and _____ power.

If the number of new full members joining had been very large and there was no differentiation between new and longer-term members, the value of the windfall paid to full members could have decreased. This could have pushed longer-term full members to seek to lobby or influence John Maxwell and his management team to distinguish between long- and short-term members.

Heading _____

The merchant bank Schroders was a category _____stakeholder, as it had relatively little interest in whether the AA finally decided to demutualise. However, as corporate adviser to the AA, it was relatively powerful as it was able to advise and potentially influence John Maxwell and his management team.

Heading _____

The category _____ stakeholders, those with _____ interest and _____power in the demutualisation issue, included associate members and employees. The associate members clearly had a _____ interest in whether or not the AA decided to demutualise. The primary concerns for associate members were the effect of demutualisation on the services they received and the cost of associate membership. However, as non-voting members, associates had _____power to influence the outcome of any ballot on demutualisation. Equally, employees had a _____ interest in the future of the AA and would be concerned as to the effects of demutualisation. Potential effects of demutualisation could have included the AA becoming more competitive and this being achieved via cost cutting and job losses. However, employees had no direct role in the ballot and would ultimately have to accept its outcome.

However, also with _____ interest and _____ power were other stakeholders like potential bidders such as Ford and competitors like Direct Line and Green Flag. These were external stakeholders with a _____ interest in what the AA would eventually decide to do, as their business and the marketplace in which they operated would be directly influenced by that decision.

Heading _____

The key players were the Director-General of the AA and his immediate management team carrying out the strategic review, as well as the full members of the AA. John Maxwell and his management team were key players with _____ power and _____ interest, as their planning and decision making would determine their future with the AA, the future of the AA, the future of those who worked for the AA, and the future of AA members. The full members would collectively decide whether the AA would demutualise. They might have chosen to support any demutualisation recommendations made by John Maxwell and his team, or to reject them in favour of a bidder, such as Ford, buying the AA.

(Source: based on Capon, 2004, *Understanding Organisational Context*, Prentice Hall, pp. 390–2)

Text 2.16

Text	Notes
Paragraph 1 **The AA and stakeholders with high power and high interest (category D)** The key players were the Director-General of the AA and his immediate management team carrying out the strategic review, as well as the full members of the AA. John Maxwell and his management team were key players with high power and high interest, as their planning and decision making would determine their future with the AA, the future of the AA, the future of those who worked for the AA, and the future of AA members. The full members would collectively decide whether the AA would demutualise. They might have chosen to support any demutualisation recommendations made by John Maxwell and his team, or to reject them in favour of a bidder, such as Ford, buying the AA.	

Paragraph 2

The AA and stakeholders with high power and low interest (category C)

The merchant bank Schroders was a category C stakeholder, as it had relatively little interest in whether the AA finally decided to demutualise. However, as corporate adviser to the AA, it was relatively powerful as it was able to advise and potentially influence John Maxwell and his management team.

Paragraph 3

The AA and stakeholders with low power and high interest (category B)

The category B stakeholders, those with high interest and low power in the demutualisation issue, included associate members and employees. The associate members clearly had a high interest in whether or not the AA decided to demutualise. The primary concerns for associate members were the effect of demutualisation on the services they received and the cost of associate membership. However, as non-voting members, associates had no direct power to influence the outcome of any ballot on demutualisation. Equally, employees had a high interest in the future of the AA and would be concerned as to the effects of demutualisation.

Potential effects of demutualisation could have included the AA becoming more competitive and this being achieved via cost cutting and job losses. However, employees had no direct role in the ballot and would ultimately have to accept its outcome.

Paragraph 4

However, also with high interest and low power were other stakeholders like potential bidders such as Ford and competitors like Direct Line and Green Flag. These were external stakeholders with a great deal of interest in what the AA would eventually decide to do, as their business and the marketplace in which they operated would be directly influenced by that decision.

Paragraph 5

The AA and stakeholders with low power and low interest (category A)

The category A stakeholders are those with low power and low interest. For the AA, non-members fell into this category. They were unable to receive breakdown services from the organisation and had no influence over its demutualisation decision. However, it should be recognised that stakeholders' power and influence can alter over time. The opportunity of a £200–250 windfall might have encouraged some non-members to become members and move to category D, high interest and high power.

Paragraph 6

If the number of new full members joining had been very large and there was no differentiation between new and longer-term members, the value of the windfall paid to full members could have decreased. This could have pushed longer-term full members to seek to lobby or influence John Maxwell and his management team to distinguish between long- and short-term members.

(Source: Capon, 2004, *Understanding Organisational Context*, Prentice Hall, pp. 389–92)

Text 2.17

Use the stakeholder model of the business environment to analyse the main influences on Nike evident in the case study

Business does not operate in a vacuum. There is always an environment, 'a set of external conditions under which a business organisation exists and operates' (Lucas, 2000, p.5). When considering a business, its environment, and the way in which they influence each other, it is useful to have a 'model', which is a simplified picture of the context in which events are taking place. A model helps to identify external influences on a business and analyse their effects on the behaviour of the business.

The model which will be used in this essay is the stakeholder model. This model 'allows us to view the various individuals and power groups with interests in the organisation – stakeholders – attempting to exert influence' (Lucas, 2000, p.60). The concepts of influence and power are central to this model. It analyses who has an interest – a 'stake' – in how a business behaves, and who actually has the power to exert an effective influence. This model will be used to analyse the influences on the large multi-national corporation, Nike, as shown in the case study 'Keep on running; the training shoe business' (Sturges, 2000).

The case study gives several instances of the importance to Nike of consumers, a significant stakeholder group. This group exert a powerful influence over the business behaviour of the company because of their spending power – over £1 billion was spent on training shoes in the UK in 1998 (Sturges, 2000, p.11). An example of consumer influence is the 'pyramid segmentation' system (Gordon, OU, video), which ensures that a design is made available only to a very exclusive group of consumers at first, and then withdrawn for several months before being marketed more broadly. ... This influential group must be won over in order to make the shoe desirable to the larger consumer group with the financial power.

The power of the consumer to influence the business behaviour of Nike is also seen in the issue of corporate responsibility. The case study describes how Nike and other trainer companies initially responded to criticism of working conditions in Indonesia 'by claiming that the issue was the responsibility of their subcontractors' (Sturges, 2000, p.30). As consumers took an increasing interest in Nike's business practices in the third world, they exerted influence on the company. By the end of the 1990's corporate responsibility was 'perceived as an important means of establishing their credibility with their customers, current and future, as they attempt to expand sales of their product throughout the world' (Sturges, 2000, p.31).

[...]

The group of employees is another stakeholder exerting influence on Nike, with a stark contrast between the direct employees in the West and the subcontracted workers in the third world. The factory workers have virtually no power over policy decisions. 'It is no coincidence, it is argued, that the manufacture of training shoes takes place in countries such as Indonesia and China which have repressive governments and weak labour unions' (Sturges, 2000, p.28). Unfortunately, these unskilled workers are seen as easily replaceable, unlike the cosseted team in the United States. It was part of Nike's original successful strategy to recognise that value is added to shoes not in the manufacturing, but in the design and marketing (Sturges, 2000, p.21). The small number of employees with those skills give Nike an edge with the consumer. These people have influence within the company.

When the stakeholder model is used to analyse the influences on Nike evident in the case study, the most influential group appears to be the consumers. Other models would perhaps highlight different elements in the business environment. One such model is the STEP checklist, which places external influences into four categories – social, technological, economic and political (Armson *et al.*, 2000, p.12). The situation of sub-contracted workers might have more prominence in Nike's environment if one looked from a political viewpoint. The trainer companies 'were forced to respond when the subject was drawn to the attention of the US State Department' (Sturges, 2000, p.30). Here is an influence which the stakeholder model does not emphasise.

When looking from an economic viewpoint, shareholders would become more prominent. Nike needs capital investment to sustain its success, and shareholders must be given a profit. Much of the Nike image involves masking the profit motive and portraying a company dealing in life-styles, but the underlying aim is still 'to *boost the worth* of their products by attaching social, cultural and emotional values to them' (Sturges, 2000, p.33, my italics). As Phil Knight says, 'When you go to buy a shoe, you're not buying one from each company, you're going to buy one pair. We're going to try as hard as we can to make that shoe Nike' (OU video). The power of the shareholders, and the continual imperative to make large profits which influences every business decision made by Nike, is clearer when the STEP model focuses attention on economics.

To conclude, the case study presents a variety of influences on Nike. Skilled employees, competitors and governments cannot be ignored and have a degree of influence. The most influential stakeholder groups are shareholders and consumers, who keep Nike constantly battling for the markets – 'innovate or die' (Riley, OU video).

References

Armson, R., Martin, J., Carr, S., Spear, R. and Walsh, T. (2000) 'Identifying Environmental Issues', in Lucas, M. (ed.) *Understanding Business: Environments*, London, Routledge / The Open University.

Farris, Nelson, Nike Director of Corporate Education, on B200, Understanding Business Behaviour Video (2000) 'Keep on running: the training shoe business', VC1188, The Open University Business School, Milton Keynes.

Gordon, Deedee, Trend Forecasting Consultant, on B200 Understanding Business Behaviour Video, (2000) 'Keep on running: the training shoe business', VC1188, The Open University Business School, Milton Keynes.

Lucas, M. (2000) *Environments. Module 1 Study Guide*, The Open University Business School, Milton Keynes.

Riley, Ray, Design Director for New Business, Nike, on B200, Understanding Business Behaviour Video (2000) 'Keep on running: the training shoe business', VC1188, The Open University Business School, Milton Keynes.

Sturges, Jane. (2000) 'Keep on running: the training shoe business', The Open University Business School, Milton Keynes.

(Source: adapted from OU Business School student assignment)

Session 3 resources

Text 3.1

Debt in the UK and the role of credit reference agencies

Paragraph 1

These days, people can apply for credit from almost anywhere. You can apply over the internet, by telephone, in a shop, supermarket, motorway service station or in a shopping centre. Direct marketing campaigns drop 'not-to-be-missed' offers through our doors on a daily basis. All of this pressure on people to consume invariably means that they need to borrow money in order to buy the goods and services that they need and they think they need.

Paragraph 2

There are developments on the horizon which may mean that spending will rise even further. Until recently, use of the internet for commerce has been limited. US$100 billion was spent online by US consumers in the past 12 months – which amounts to only 2.6% of the $3.9 trillion in US retail sales. Only 54% of US adults who use the Web have bought stuff there, according to 2003 census data. This has been because of slow broadband penetration, security fears and the hassle of having to rummage for a credit card when it is time to check out. Half of all online shopping carts are abandoned at checkout and half of 5000 web users polled recently by Gartner said they worry about data theft.

Paragraph 3

This could all change with the arrival of a new service called Bill Me Later. This is the internet equivalent of asking the neighbourhood grocer to give you credit. Instead of using a credit card number at checkout, a shopper clicks on the Bill Me Later button and is greeted as if the service already knows them; it asks for the last four digits of their Social Security number and their date of birth. If a shopper's credit is good, Bill Me Later pays the merchant and sends the shopper a bill within two weeks. One can pay right away or later, with interest. What is the impact on spending? On Walmart. com's checkout page, Bill Me Later gets top billing of all credit payment options. Bradford Matson, head of marketing at discount luxury goods site Bluefly.com, says he launched Bill Me Later's service a year ago and says it boosted his sales. Bluefly customers typically shop three times a year at the site, but its Bill Me Later customers buy four times a year. Their average order value is also 15% higher.

Paragraph 4

Whether or not people borrow and how much depends on not only their financial requirements and developments in technology but also their attitudes to debt. For example, in contrast to the UK's insatiable appetite for taking on debt, many major European countries have a culture of saving, and some, such as France and Germany, are particularly debt averse.

Paragraph 5

So what are the wider social attitudes to debt? An Index developed by BMRB has been measuring the British population's responses to the statement 'I don't like the idea of being in debt' since 1987. Overall broad agreement with the statement has stayed steadfastly at between 80 and 85% of the adult population throughout the years since then but there is evidence that there has been an underlying softening of attitudes which is more prevalent among some sub-groups than others and which may be a pragmatic response to growing debt levels.

Paragraph 6

There can be little doubt that the plethora of publicity surrounding the nation's private debt levels has helped to ease a greater number of people into some sort of comfort zone based on the fact that they are not as unusual as they might first have thought. However, the prospect of a cooling in the house price market (and the removal of that particular safety blanket) may well cause the nation to begin to think differently.

Paragraph 7

The wider impact of this change in attitudes can be seen from national economic statistics. Individuals in the UK have an average of £3175 unsecured debt, more than double that in the rest of western Europe, according to research from independent analyst Datamonitor.

Paragraph 8

Just as consumers have become more comfortable with the idea of taking on debt, the same applies to their attitudes to declaring bankruptcy, when levels of debt become too high and they find that they are not able to make payments to their creditors. Such measures can mean that the individual is able to 'walk away' from their debts without having to pay them off, however, they may not be able to take on debt in the future.

Paragraph 9

As personal insolvencies hit another record high, new attitudes are driving the rise in the latest insolvency statistics. Rather than suffer in debt people are seeking a remedy to their debt anxieties. Bev Budsworth of The Debt Advisor says, 'Attitudes have changed towards debt fuelled by the unrealistic lifestyle aspirations from glossy magazines and TV makeover programmes. Twenty-five years ago, lifestyles were different and views towards money have subtly changed. Where credit was seen as debt, debt is now seen as credit, as a way of living the celebrity lifestyle.'

[...]

Paragraph 10

There are three credit reference agencies – Experian, Equifax and Callcredit – and they all hold information gleaned from the electoral roll such as individuals' address details and the names of others who live at the property. They also hold on file details of any County Court Judgments and bankruptcies. Alongside that will be information passed on to them from various banks and building societies about an individual's payment history for cards, loans, mortgages, etc. that you already have. The developments in technology mean that such agencies are better able than ever to gather large amounts of data on individuals, from a variety of different sources; indeed, their records on individuals are updated daily.

Paragraph 11

Another factor fuelling the need for credit references has been the growth of e-commerce where sales are projected to carry on growing robustly. During 2006, British retailers have made larger investments than ever before in their online services, in response to their customers' enthusiasm for them. The common availability of broadband has allowed retailers to present much higher quality product photographs and images – which are now often scaleable – and even explanatory videos. Real time details of stock availability have become the norm. Delivery services are being transformed; for example, specific delivery time slots are becoming available for a growing number of non-food items, which is great news for people who are normally out during the day.

Paragraph 12

The boom in e-commerce has meant that Experian has had to introduce new technologies. Ordering a credit report is now simpler and quicker than ever. Consumer education also has to evolve with technology. Experian's website contains lots of information about credit reports and gives consumers online answers to their questions.

References

www.dmnews.com/cms/dm-news/catalog-retail/34141.html

www.fool.co.uk/school/2006/sch060123.htm

www.forbes.com/free_forbes/2006/1211/068.html?partner=yahoomag

www.fsa.gov.uk/consumer/04_CREDIT_DEBT/mn_lender_info.html

www.imrg.org/ItemDetail.aspx?clg=InfoItems&cid=NewStuff&pid=doc_ Senate_Christmas_Statement_06&language=en-GB

www.marketresearchworld.net/index.php? option=content&task=view&id=643&Itemid=

www.screenpages.com/archives/000270.html

www.thedebtadvisor.co.uk/pdfs/3rd-february-2006.pdf

http://thescotsman.scotsman.com/business.cfm?id=1432912006

(Source: Haider Ali, 2007, Open University Business School, Milton Keynes)

Text 3.2

Minding the Gap: the decline and recovery of a clothing company

Foundations of The Gap

Gap Inc. is a specialist clothing retailer which operates stores selling casual apparel, personal care and other accessories under the Gap brand and also under the Banana Republic and Old Navy brands. The company designs virtually all of its products, which in turn are manufactured by independent sources, and sells them under its brand names through its own stores, via catalogue and online.

The Gap story began in 1969, in Berkeley, California. Don Fisher, a real estate developer with a bohemian streak, opened a store with his wife, Doris, selling bell-bottom Levi's. The Generation Gap, as it was then called, quickly became the place to buy your jeans. By the 1980s, Gap had expanded into a cult empire, selling laid-back west coast campus style to baby boomers for whom Gap khakis made them feel, in some vague way, closer to their cool, carefree 1969 selves.

A landmark advertising campaign in the late 1980s featured American heroes from Miles Davis to Marilyn Monroe in their own khakis, when being photographed by Herb Ritts or Annie Liebowitz for Vanity Fair. Contemporary stars returned the compliment by adopting en masse a uniform of Gap black T-shirt and khakis. This became the modern equivalent of Levi's and a white shirt: the fashionable way to portray oneself as above fashion. Later on, in the 1990s, Gap found a natural constituency amongst the dot.commers, its clothes as much a part of the start-up iconography as brightly coloured laptops and takeaway latte. And as the baby boomers grew up, the Gap family grew with them: GapKids and BabyGap were born in 1986 and 1990 respectively.

The year 2000, however, appeared to mark a turning point in the fortunes of Gap Inc. Sales and profitability began to decline and the downward trends continued throughout the next 3 years despite all attempts by the senior management to turn them around. In 2002 this culminated in a change of Chief Executive Officer (CEO). The much respected Millard Drexler retired after 19 years at Gap Inc. to be replaced by Paul Pressler, a former executive at Disney Corporation. The question remains whether this change 'at the helm' will stimulate Gap's recovery?

[...]

How Gap sees itself: structure and processes

From its US headquarters in San Francisco, Gap Inc. operates more than 4200 stores in US, Canada, France, Germany, Japan and UK alongside product development offices in New York and distribution operations and offices, 'coordinating sourcing activities around the globe'. It employs approximately 165,000 people.

[...]

A good company to work for?

Gap Inc. is proud of the range of benefits and support it offers to its staff, in addition to the competitive salaries and bonuses. These include:

- Employee Health & Well-being Programme which includes private healthcare arrangements, a 24 hour 'Nurseline', staff insurance for a range of circumstances and a personal counselling service

- Financial assistance for new homes, moving and relocation, travel and study

- Career Planning including an internal placement scheme and staff e-learning resources

- Family Support Programme offering pre-natal risk assessment, enabling new parents to take paid time off on the birth or adoption of their child, contributing to dependent care costs and of course providing gifts and discounts on babyGap merchandise.

Gap also encourage their staff to engage in volunteer work for community-based organizations by providing paid time-off and matching donations to the organizations.

In 2002 the company was ranked number 2 out of the top 25 by the non-profit organization, Professional Business Women of California (PBWC) for its support for women employees. This was based on a range of criteria including the percentages of women in executive and corporate officer positions, and sitting on the board of directors. It backs up its philosophy of diversity and equal opportunity with a policy of zero tolerance for discriminatory behaviour on any grounds.

Sourcing of manufactured goods

Despite having what they claim is a 'global reach', Gap do not own or operate any factories for the manufacture of garments. In 2002 their clothing was produced in around 3000 factories in over 50 countries. They claim that 'Sourcing our product with a variety of vendors gives greater flexibility when fashion dictates the use of different fabrics, techniques or expertise' ('Beyond the Label' factsheet from Gap.com). This international network of manufacturers is controlled via rigorous processes of prior vetting and monitoring against company standards. Some of these standards relate to quality assurance and production engineering – ensuring that a manufacturer meets the required quality standards and has the capacity to accept a particular order – while others relate to Gap's corporate ethical values. The framework for this is set out in a Code of Vendor Conduct which Gap first produced in the early 1990s in response to criticisms of 'sweat-shop' labour conditions amongst some of its vendors. As the Guardian later published:

> The shine was first tarnished in 1992, when an American reporter stumbled upon a factory in Saipan, in the Pacific, where Gap clothes were being produced by a subcontractor who, unknown to Gap, was hiring Chinese labourers for 80-hour weeks at less than $2 an hour. The company quickly denounced and sacked the contractor, but this was still unwelcome publicity for an organisation with native

grasses planted on the roof of its San Francisco headquarters for eco-friendly insulation, and baby-friendly quiet rooms for nursing mothers.

(The Guardian, 23/11/01)

As a result Gap Inc. produced the Code as a means of influencing working conditions and management practices in their vendor organizations.

The monitoring and evaluation of Gap-approved garment producers is conducted by a multi-national team of Vendor Compliance Officers (VCOs) who are part of Gap Inc.'s Global Compliance Team based in San Francisco. They are drawn from a variety of backgrounds such as the law, academia and the voluntary sector. Their role encompasses a range of activities including conducting routine site visits, investigations of reported breaches of the Code, enforcing corrective action on health and safety, acting as advocate for a vendor's employee and negotiating improvement programmes with vendors. Their objective is to ensure Gap Inc.'s vendor organizations understand the company's ethical commitments and that they abide by them as closely as possible allowing for differences in cultural context. Gap's approach is to encourage continuous improvement but where serious breaches of the Code of Conduct or a pattern of non-compliance occur, they suspend or terminate business with the vendor. In 2002 they terminated business with vendors owning 120 factories around the world.

Despite this, the company came in for renewed criticism from development campaigners in 2002. The campaign group Africa Forum joined together with Unite, the international union of textile workers, to publicise and denounce what they saw as 'abusive working conditions' – a combination of long hours, low pay, health hazards and exploitative management practice – amongst Gap's suppliers in at least six countries. In a press release the campaigners called for a consumer boycott during the run-up to Christmas 2002.

Trends in the European clothing retail sector

Gap's retail operations extend to UK, Germany and France, three of Europe's top four clothes-buying nations, who together generate around 55% of clothing retail sales in Europe. Since 1996, however, the European market has been experiencing a significant restructuring associated with the following factors:

- A decline in the proportion of consumer spending on clothing e.g. in Germany clothing represented 6.3% of total consumer spending in 1990 but had declined to 4.9% in 1998
- Trends in consumer taste away from uniformity and towards diversity
- Increased competition in clothing 'basics' from lower priced chains and supermarket/hypermarket retailers
- A continuation in the longer term trend toward industry concentration i.e. a decreasing number of retailers supplying the market.

This has led to increasingly intense competition across Europe which led to downward pressure on prices. In 1999 clothing prices across Europe rose by only 0.2%. This pressure was particularly marked in the UK where prices fell by 5.2% in 1999 and by a further 8.5% in 2000. While low value clothing chains, such as Matalan in the UK and Primark in Ireland, and supermarkets/hypermarkets have performed strongly in the midst of this, the middle market providers, such as the UK-based Marks & Spencer and the German-Dutch C&A chain have seen their market shares and profits squeezed. Marks & Spencer for example saw a decline in their market share in Europe from 16% to 11% between 1996 and 1999. Another UK-based retailer, Next plc, decided to focus entirely on their domestic market and closed down all outlets outside the UK.

Gap goes into decline?

After a 16 year period of sustained growth, Gap experienced a serious decline in sales and profits during 2000. This was first reported in the business press during autumn 2000. The Guardian (18th November, 2000) reported as follows:

> The chain credited with dressing the world in chinos and baseball caps has had a bad year. A string of profits warnings and disappointing sales figures since the spring wiped about $25bn from its stock market value. Last week, after announcing that third-quarter profits had fallen 41%, the shares were trading at about $24, down from a 52-week high of $53.75 reached in April. Sales of the group's three domestic brands – Gap, Old Navy and Banana Republic – have all fallen in the past few months, as they have in the company's rapidly expanding international stores.

Initially it was felt that this was due to the broader economic slowdown in the US, in turn sparked by a slump in the stock market and rises in interest rates combined with long-standing high levels of debt amongst American consumers. This was thought to affect sales in the clothing retail sector particularly sharply. In one assessment of the state of the sector, Wendy Liebmann, president of WSL Strategic Retail, a firm of market analysts, said: 'A combination of the economy and the elections are making consumers nervous. That sort of nervousness hits the retail sector across the board, but it hits apparel first.'

While The Gap was not the only clothing company to have suffered from the downturn in consumer confidence, others seemed relatively unscathed. Low-cost operators such as Wal-Mart, a direct competitor to Old Navy, were continuing to do well. For Gap however, the changing economic conditions merely highlighted internal problems of 'uninspiring merchandise and poor management'.

After initially blaming a combination of the economic slowdown and bad weather earlier in the year, by September executives were admitting to 'inventory problems, heavy markdowns and a dispiriting advertising campaign which focused on in-store promotions rather than brand-building slots on television.' Analysts knew things were bad when, during the busy back-to-school period, the company was offering 20% discounts. Gap seldom promotes cut-price offers. The company moved quickly to clear up the inventory problems which had led to late deliveries and began a new television advertising campaign in November, 2000. It also recruited new heads of marketing for Banana Republic and Old Navy.

Most significantly however, many stock market analysts criticized the company for losing sight of its core business. They believed the company had made a mistake by trying to attract teenagers looking for trendy clothes. 'Gap moved away from its core strengths and it needs to get them back,' said one US retail analyst. In an address to the company's shareholders, Mickey Drexler, the chief executive, assured them that 'In spite of the short term screw-ups we've been through, ... we still have three incredibly strong, powerful brands we feel have exciting long term opportunities.' Shareholders were critical of the management team, but at that stage stopped short of demanding any serious reorganisation. The board also retained the backing of the founding Fisher family, which still owned 30% of the company. The year ended with analysts, such as Wendy Liebmann, backing Drexler's optimistic assessment of the longer term. 'Gap goes through four- or five-year cycles when, after incredible highs, everybody has enough casual stuff. Then, all at once, Gap comes up with something and it starts again.'

By Christmas 2001 however, it had become evident that Gap was facing more fundamental problems. As the Guardian (23rd November, 2001) reported, 'The neatly folded piles of scarlet hoodies arranged to catch the eye of passers-by still attract a respectable crowd, but behind the scenes the company acknowledges it has hit hard times. It has just announced net losses of $179m (£127m) for the third quarter. For the first time in over 10 years one of retail's most popular success stories is losing money.' In December 2001 the firm announced a worldwide drop in its annual sales of 24%.

This time Gap's senior executives felt they had to pay attention to the criticisms of their confused brand identity. Around a thousand staff were laid off in July 2001, despite the fact that denim and corduroy, two staples of the Gap look, had been very much in fashion that year. 'We lost sight of our brand positioning. We let ourselves get too swept up in trends. We lost focus,' a Gap spokesperson was quoted as saying. In the wake of further economic uncertainty post-September 11, 'focus' was the buzzword in retail. It was perceived as a time to concentrate on core strengths to weather the storm. But to some Gap's troubles indicated that 'at 32, Gap appears to have hit an early mid-life crisis, and no one knows quite where it will end.'

Change of CEO and fortunes?

In September 2002 in the wake of 29 months consecutive decline in sales and a record low of $8.35 in the share price, Gap Inc. replaced their CEO of 19 years, Millard Drexler, with newcomer Paul Pressler. Pressler had an impressive track record in marketing, latterly running Disney Corp's theme parks. Pressler launched his first new products for Gap in a blaze of publicity in August 2003. The company had signed two of the US' biggest pop music stars, Madonna and Missy Elliot, to appear in their advertisements. Even at that stage stock market confidence had improved to such an extent that the share price had recovered to $18 – still less than half its value ($36.75) in May 2000, before the decline had begun. Nevertheless it was seen as a step in the right direction.

(Source: OU Business School case study, 2004)

Text 3.3

Use the stakeholder model of business environments to critically examine the external environment of Gap Inc., as outlined in the case study

Text	Notes
Gap stakeholders. Because the nature of the stakes held by each stakeholder differs from the next, it is logical to assume that their interests sometimes conflict. Based on the case study, this short essay will identify Gap's main stakeholders and explain the nature of their stakes before critically examining the abilities of each to influence Gap Inc.	The essay identifies the main stakeholder of Gap.
Gap stakeholders	
The stakeholder model enables us to view various individuals and power groups who have an interest in the organisation. The following principal stakeholders have been identified from the Gap case study: Donald Fisher and family Other shareholders CEO Board of directors Employees Associates, including suppliers, manufacturers, customers Non-profit organisations Special interest groups Vendor compliance officers	This identifies Gap's main stakeholders.
How much influence in their relationship with the company to make over a thousand staff redundant [...] demonstrating that shareholders are more powerful stakeholders than employees. When performance is poor, management are accountable to shareholders, not employees and will make such decisions accordingly. Donald Fisher, Gap's main shareholder chose not to make changes at the top when Gap's problems were first bought to light, but he could have had he so wished. Shareholders might therefore be seen as the most powerful stakeholders. This is not surprising; after all, they own the company.	

Suppliers seek profitable business with Gap. Gap operates in a highly competitive global environment. For this reason, Gap's suppliers and manufacturers are able to exert little influence in their relationship with the company. If Gap is unsatisfied with the way its suppliers conduct their business practices for example, it can simply outsource its manufacturing to a competitor in a different country (pp.14–15). Likewise, it is Gap's requirement that relationships with manufacturers remain flexible, not vice versa.

'Vendor compliance' officers exist as stakeholders to ensure that the production standards are maintained and moral codes of conduct to which Gap subscribes are not breached. They have a good deal of influence over the way the company sources its manufacturing and can influence the choice of supplier and manufacturer.

Special interest groups which include not-for-profit organisations are on the periphery of Gap's external environment in terms of their formal involvement with the company. Nevertheless, these organisations have their own agenda and use the media to highlight their agenda and influence the way the company does business (pp.12–13). In this respect, well organised and connected organisations on the periphery are relatively powerful.

Customer decisions to buy are based on a number of factors including economic climate, marketing and price. In many respects, customers are the most powerful stakeholder. They have the power to determine whether Gap exists as an organisation or not.

However, in reality, the consumer has little say in the company decision making unless, of course, other factors serve to highlight problems. The aforementioned non-profit organisation's highlighting of exploitation in developing countries by Gap's suppliers for example may prompt consumers to alter their spending habits with Gap.

Conclusion

Using the stakeholder model, Gap's principal stakeholders were identified and the nature of their stakes explained. The external environment was shown to be a potential arena for conflict, where stakeholders compete for influence. It was suggested that shareholders were the dominant stakeholders because senior management was accountable to them. Meanwhile, associates such as manufacturers and suppliers are the weakest players. The intensely competitive environment in which they operate ensures that Gap always holds the upper hand in these relationships. Finally, it was suggested that customers hold the key to Gap's fortunes but were unlikely to use their power unless groups such as nonprofit organisations or the media on the periphery enlightened customers to Gap's business practices.

This summarises the points made in the previous paragraphs.

(Source: Haider Ali, 2007, Open University Business School, Milton Keynes)

Text 3.4

Copper price rises in UK after Chile strike

BHP Billiton PLC's Chilean workers went on strike at Escondida, the world's biggest copper mine, following a dispute over wages that increased prices for the metal yesterday in London.

Workers at the mine in northern Chile began the walkout yesterday morning after management failed to meet demands to boost wages almost 17 per cent, said Pedro Marin, a spokesman for the union. Escondida accounted for 8.5 per cent of copper mined in 2005.

'Everything at the mine is stopped,' Marin said, in a telephone interview from near the city of Antofagasta, Chile.

The strike halted production and will keep output depressed even as the company uses contractors to run equipment, Marin said. Mauro Valdes, a spokesman for BHP Billiton, the world's largest mining company, said the strike has cut processing capacity by about 60 per cent and that the company is tapping stockpiles of ore to keep equipment running.

Speculation that the protest will disrupt supplies buoyed prices on the London Metals Exchange, where copper rose $70 (US), or 0.9 per cent, to $7,930 a tonne. In New York, copper's slide on speculation stockpiles will enable the mine to weather a strike. Copper for delivery in September fell 2.2 cents, or 0.6 per cent, to $3.6105 a pound on the New York Mercantile Exchange.

Workers at BHP Billiton, along with miner Codelco, are seeking wage increases in Chile after copper prices more than doubled in a year.

The strike is the second at Escondida since 1997. Workers last went on strike in August 2003, a protest that lasted less than a day. Copper prices have more than tripled since then.

The union on Aug. 4 rejected a management offer for a salary increase of 3 percentage points above the inflation rate, which was 3.8 per cent annually in July, and for a bonus of 8.5 million pesos ($17,510 Canadian) per worker.

The union, called Escondida's Workers' Union Number 1, wants a wage increase of 13 percentage points above inflation and a bonus of 16 million pesos per worker. Workers on average earn about 650,000 pesos ($1,330) per month, said Cipriano Zuluaga, a union director. The union said its 2,052 members represent about 94 per cent of the mine's workers. According to Escondida's management, the union represents 70 per cent of the mine's workers.

Prices have surged from a 14-year low in 2001 of 60.35 cents (US) a pound. China, the world's biggest copper user, has increased purchases of copper wire and pipe, reducing global stockpiles of the metal.

The strike 'creates more tightness in the market,' said Mark Pervan, an analyst at Daiwa Securities SMBC, in Melbourne.

Escondida accounts for almost a fourth of Chile's total copper production. BHP Billiton, which owns 57.5 per cent of Escondida, gets about a fifth of its profit from the mine, according to estimates by ABN Amro Australia Ltd. Escondida was generating $1 million (US) an hour in net operating profit after tax for BHP Billiton in May, according to a May 5 note from Peter O'Connor and Jeremy Gray, analysts at Credit Suisse Group. Rio Tinto, which owns 30 per cent of the mine, got 18.5 per cent of its record first-half profit from Escondida.

State-owned Codelco, meanwhile, is dealing with an accident at its Chuquicamata mining complex, which may result in a loss of up to 960 tonnes per day. In Canada, Inco Ltd's Voisey's Bay project in Newfoundland is in the midst of a job action after union and management failed to agree on wages and benefits.

(Source: Walsh, H., 2006, *The Toronto Star*, 8 August)

Text 3.5

Escondida stakeholder analysis

The case presents the situation at a copper mine in Chile. The mine appears to be a joint venture between two western companies, BHP Billiton and Rio Tinto and Codelco, the Chilean state mining company. The key issue addressed by the case is the strike being mounted by workers for better pay in the face of rising prices for the mine's output, which is copper. Chile is one of the world's major producers of copper and reference is also made in the case to China which is one of the largest consumers.

High interest and high power stakeholders

These are the stakeholders who have a high level of interest in the strike and also a high level of power in being able to influence the outcome.

In this category we could place the following groups. The 'Escondida's workers' union Number 1' derives its power from the fact that it represents the workers and would also have a high level of interest in resolving the situation. However, the level of power that it enjoys seems to be disputed by BHP Billiton who claim that rather than representing 94% of workers it actually represents 70%.

The other party in the negotiation would be the employers and they would be represented by the mine owners who are BHP Billiton and Codelco. These organisations would also have a high level of interest in seeing the dispute resolved. In BHP Billiton's case, this would be because the mine represents a significant proportion of its total profits. In the case of Codelco the interest would be because of the possible impact on the rest of the Chilean mining industry. Also having a high level of interest but perhaps less power would be Rio Tinto which has a share in the mine (which is slightly more than half of that of BHP Billiton).

It should be noted that the actual level of power enjoyed by Rio Tinto would depend on the nature of the agreements entered into by the three joint venture partners. Indeed, while they may have a high level of interest in the outcome, the level of power enjoyed by the actual management of the mine will depend on the level of central control exerted by the three mine owners.

Low power and high interest

In terms of stakeholders with low power and a high level of interest, the group in this category would be individual workers – because on their own these people would have very little ability to exert any influence on the organisation. Their power is derived by being able to negotiate on a collective basis.

Low power and low interest

The case makes reference to contractors being used to run the equipment. They may have an interest in the outcome in so far as it influences their work, but there seems to be no explicit cause for their being able to exercise any power.

The case mentions that China is the world's largest buyer of copper and we can only assume that it may have an interest and power in the outcome, because there is no reference to any power being exercised. Inference can be made about high interest, because of the country's position as a copper consumer. Similarly, although only passing reference is made to Chile as a country, one would assume that the government of the country has a high level of interest in the outcome but the level of power it can exert will depend on its relationship with Codelco (the state copper producer).

(Source: Haider Ali, 2007, Open University Business School, Milton Keynes)

Session 4 resources

Text 4.1

From competition to collaboration

Competition in the Scottish electronics industry for skilled technicians is famously intense and in the early 1990s recruitment problems were getting out of hand. 'We were basically poaching from each other and pushing salaries up. It was becoming a vicious circle,' says Morag McKelvie, a personnel manager at NEC semiconductors.

The idea then that managers from competing companies would start working together to solve the skills shortage would have seemed incredible, she says. Russell Pryde, manager of ... one of Scotland's local enterprise councils, agrees. 'I don't think they would have sat in the same room together.'

But in a striking turnaround, a number of competitors have embarked on an unprecedented degree of cooperation on training over the past two years. Yesterday, their innovative approach was recognised when ... they received a special training award from the Institute of Personnel and Development at the National Training Awards, organised by the Department for Education and Employment.

(Source: Vanessa Houlder, 1997, 'Alternative to poaching: how companies can collaborate to beat skills shortages', *Financial Times*, 13 February, adapted from Capon)

Text 4.2

Putting the fizz back into Coke

Marketing chiefs at Coca-Cola's head office in Atlanta are said to be working on a vanilla-favoured version of its core soft drink, described as the biggest innovation in 20 years for the world-recognised brand.

The development is one of several strategies designed to put some *fizz* back into Coke.

With consumers becoming more health conscious, both Coca-Cola and Pepsi-Co – who dominate the cola market worldwide – have seen steadily falling sales of their best-known products since the 1980s. The diet version of both brands improved sales but not by enough to make up the deficit.

Uncertainties surrounding its internal restructuring caused Coca-Cola a further setback over the last two years. During this period it lost 0.4% of its US market share, which fell to 43.7%, whilst Pepsi-Co's market share increased by 0.2 to 31.6%.

Sweet fizzy drinks such as cola are losing sales to plain bottled water, an area which both Coca-Cola and Pepsi-Co have been moving into in recent years. But Pepsi has moved more quickly. It was faster to spot the growth area than its competitor and is ranked number two in the US bottled water market after Perrier. Coke lies third.

Yet Coca-Cola's fortunes are starting to show small signs of improvement. The company was encouraged by its sponsorship of the Winter Olympics, an event that gained wide publicity in the USA. Its marketing chiefs speak of the possibility of a similar sponsorship deal within the next two years. Coca-Cola's shares are currently worth half their 1998 price but renewed confidence in the company is reflected in a gradual increase in their value since the beginning of the year.

(Source: based on *The Guardian*, 2 April 2002, from *Cobuild Business Vocabulary in Practice*, 2005, p. 209, London, HarperCollins)

Text 4.3

The following is a SWOT analysis based on the case study provided of Coca-Cola.

Coca-Cola has a number of strengths, possibly one of the most important of which is its globally recognised brand. Very often the generic drink of 'cola' is referred to by many people as "Coke" which is obviously a huge benefit to the Coca-Cola company when customers are purchasing this type of product. This recognisable brand helps make Coca-Cola the market leader with a market share of 43.7% the cola business. A further strength for Coca-Cola has been the high profile sponsorship of the Winter Olympic Games. This sporting event was broadcast on millions of television sets around the world which again would help to raise the company's profile. Coca-Cola have spent a great deal of time and money in improving their range of diet products. It is the combination of these strengths that have helped to renew business confidence in Coca-Cola.

Whilst the Coca-Cola company has many strengths, it also has weaknesses. One of these is that is has suffered some uncertainty from internal restructuring. A further weakness has been that the company's share price has halved since 1998. This has been due to the general fluctuations in the stock market as well as specific concerns raised by some threats to the organisation.

Organisations such as Coca-Cola face numerous threats. Consumers are becoming much more health conscious. They face constant bombardment in the press of the issues based around the consumption of sugary, carbonated drinks and the effects such things may have on weight, tooth decay and even children's behavior and educational achievements. This change in consumer trends has led to a slight decrease in sales of Coke and an increase in popularity of mineral water. Coca-Cola's main rival Pepsi appears to be a little quicker off the mark in diversifying into this new healthier market. Their market share in "cola" with the development of their diet, sugar-free product they are also No. 2 in the bottled water market.

Whilst there are obviously threats and weakness for any organisation, there are also many new opportunities, and this is also true of Coca-Cola. The huge research and development budget has created a vanilla version of the original Coca-Cola and this is seen as the biggest innovation in 20 years. In a bid to keep up with healthier drink trends of the consumer, the company has also moved into the bottled water market. Having realised the benefits that sponsoring a world-wide sports event can bring, Coca-Cola are exploring the possibilities of future sponsorship opportunities.

(Source: OU Business School student assignment)

Text 4.4

What factors have contributed to the decline in Gap's business profits?

In 2000, following 16 years of continuous growth, the clothing merchandiser Gap began to experience a fall in both sales and profits. A number of factors may explain this change in the company's fortunes.

The general economic slowdown in the US was one of several threats that the company was facing in its external environment. This was caused by a slump in the stock market, a rise in interest rates and high levels of consumer debt. As a result, consumers were nervous, and so reduced their spending on clothing in particular. The elections and bad weather were also thought to contribute to reduced sales.

It is true that Gap had little control over these external threats. However, the fact that other clothing retailers were relatively unaffected by the same economic environment provided unwelcome competition to the company and suggested that other − internal − factors were contributing to its decline.

One of Gap's weaknesses at that time was inventory problems, leading to late deliveries. This was later resolved. Gap was also criticised for its 'uninspiring merchandise and poor management'. Company executives acknowledge that a dispiriting advertising campaign was another of its weaknesses. A further criticism was of Gap's 'confused brand identity'. An unsuccessful attempt at targeting teenagers led to accusations that it was losing sight of its core business. The company itself admitted to having 'lost focus' in this way.

Several factors would appear to have contributed to the decline in Gap's business profits. Whilst the threats in its external environment may have had an impact, they are not easy to address, and, as mentioned earlier, do not appear to have affected the company's competitors in the same way. This suggests that the company's internal problems are the main causes for its change of fortune. Although the company has a number of distinct weaknesses, its confused brand identity and loss of focus are recurrent themes and would seem to be the underlying reasons for the decline in Gap's profits in recent years.

(Source: OU Business School student assignment)

Text 4.5

Gap's next sale could be its last

Gap, the Californian-based fashion chain which started as a single shop in 1969, is by all accounts a retail phenomenon. Trading under the three labels, Gap, Old Navy and Banana Republic, its worldwide estate extends to 3,157 stores. With 130 stores, Britain is its largest international market, well ahead of Japan, Canada and France. About 153,000 people work for the company worldwide.

But after a long decline, the future of the American fashion chain is in doubt as its founders consider a sale or a break-up of the retail empire.

The company has been suffering falling like-for-like sales ever since 2004. It has admitted a 'disappointing customer response' to its products over the last few years. Its shares are less than half the level of their peak in 2000.

Such results contrast sharply with the growing popularity and success of lower-priced high street fashion chains, with which it is unable to compete.

The firm's prime high-street positions demand continuously ringing tills to pay the rent. In London, for example, Gap has a shop on Piccadilly Circus plus four more along Oxford Street.

Some suggest Gap started to lose its sharp sense of customers' tastes when long-serving chief executive Mickey Drexler left in 2002. He was replaced by a former head of Disney's theme parks, Paul Pressler, whose background is in marketing rather than fashion.

Patricia Edwards, a fund manager specialising in retail, says: 'I don't think anyone knows who they're trying to appeal to any more. Is it a 25-year-old or a 40-year-old?'

Retail analyst David Stoddard, agrees: 'If you look at its advertising and marketing, the strong message you get is that it doesn't know what it is or who we are.'

Richard Hyman, managing director of Verdict Consulting, presents another view: 'The word "fashion" denotes regular change. Gap is a business that hasn't changed sufficiently.'

Gap in the US is now focusing on its traditional strengths – jeans, T-shirts, hooded sweatshirts and khakis – to win back customers. It is also improving the quality of its fabrics.

Gap was once at the centre of sweatshop labour claims but is now greatly admired for its supply-chain management. It is also part of the charitable *Red* initiative, with 50 per cent of profits on certain items going to organisations fighting Aids in Africa.

But this may be too little, too late.

According to authoritative reports from the US, the investment bank Goldman Sachs has been hired to review all of Gap's options. One possibility would be to sell off all of its stores. Another would be to focus on developing its more successful brands, Old Navy and Banana Republic.

A Gap spokesman would neither confirm nor deny the reports. Goldman Sachs declined to comment.

If Gap were to find a buyer, the acquirer would be likely to be a private equity or other investment firm. A sale of Gap would be one of the largest buyouts ever in the retail industry. The company's current market value is $16.4bn and analysts expect a buyer would have to pay more than $18bn.

A sale of Gap would represent the end of an era for US retailing. To buy Gap, a bidder would need the backing of its founders, the Fisher family, who control more than a third of the company. But, given the value of the chain, the temptation to cash in their shares may be too great to resist.

(Source: adapted from 'Gap's next sale could be its last', 14 January 2007, *The Observer*; Andrew Clark (2007) 'Plenty of Gaps on the high street – just no shoppers to fill them', 13 January, *The Guardian*)

Session 5 resources

Extract 5.2

Supplier selection is becoming a much more important aspect of the purchasing process for many organisations. Recent trends in purchasing have seen many organisations seeking to have much closer, long-term relationships with many fewer suppliers. The term *partnership sourcing* has come into currency, and is in many respects similar to relationship marketing. With whom to have that relationship has become a vitally important decision.

The following article from the *Financial Times* explains how Toyota selects its suppliers. It was written at the time when motor manufacturing giant Toyota was setting up a production facility in Europe for the first time. It provides a fascinating insight into Japanese approaches to purchasing. Note the emphasis that Toyota place on selecting their suppliers, and the huge amount of work that they put into the selection process.

HOW TOYOTA FILTERS ITS COMPONENT SUPPLIERS

Toyota, Japan's largest car maker, is in the very last stages of whittling down to 150, from 2,000, the would-be suppliers of prototype components to its £700m UK car plant now under construction in Derbyshire.

Toyota would be desperately vulnerable to any shortcomings in its parts suppliers. It buys in 75 per cent of the value of its cars, compared with only around one half for European vehicle makers.

Yet far from 'importing' tried-and-trusted Japanese suppliers, Toyota insists that when all its Derby suppliers are disclosed they will include only a handful of Japanese companies. The vast majority, it says, will be based in the UK and continental Europe.

Toyota is paying more than lip service to maximising 'local' (EC, not just UK) content, insists Bryan Jackson, a Toyota Motor Manufacturing UK director, and Jim Robinson, its parts procurement manager who has overseen the selection process.

The point was underlined by managing director Yukihisa Hirano at a Welsh Development Agency conference last month when he talked of 'mis-perceptions' about the so-called Japanese 'transplants'.

'Toyota has never asked any Japanese companies to set up in Europe', Hirano declared. 'Among the companies from whom we have ordered prototype parts only a few are Japanese, and they were established in Europe before we made our decision to manufacture here.'

The list has been drawn up on the basis that the companies' technological abilities, investments in research and development, plant, equipment and other resources are of a standard that should allow long-term partnerships to develop with Toyota.

(Source: 'How Toyota filters its component suppliers', *Financial Times*, 10 April 1991)

(Source: Mayle, D. and Barnes, D., 2000, *Understanding Business Behaviour*, Module 3 Study Guide, pp. 41–42)

Text 5.4

Miriam's completed assignment

Gap continues to attract criticism for working conditions in some of its suppliers. Outline the key aspects of a vendor selection and monitoring process that will further Gap's long-term best interests.

[Paragraph 1]

Gap's current vendor selection policy focuses on a vendor's ability to meet product quality standards and production capacity at the right cost and also on whether they conform to ethical trading standards in line with the Code of Vendor Conduct.

[Paragraph 2]

However, this policy has not stopped criticism of the working practices of some of Gap's suppliers. It may therefore be beneficial for Gap to consider recent trends in vendor selection whereby organisations seek close long-term relationships with suppliers. These relationships are called 'partnership sourcing' and are considered mutually beneficial to both parties.

[Paragraph 3]

If Gap was interested in partnership sourcing it would have to significantly reduce the number of vendors it deals with. As Bryan Jackson, director of Toyota Motor Manufacturing UK points out 'It's rather difficult to have a relationship with 1,000 suppliers ... It's much better to have fewer, who are more closely involved' (OU Study Guide 3, p. 38).

[Paragraph 4]

Vendors could be selected to provide a larger share of the organisation's business, supplying whole product groups (one vendor for jeans; one for T-shirts, etc.). What Gap should be looking for in these suppliers is more than just their ability to deliver the product. It should also look for an understanding of company philosophy, management capability and attitude, and development capability. These are the items which the Toyota selection system, for example, pays significant attention to.

[Paragraph 5]

This form of customer-supplier relationship is obviously different to that previously experienced by Gap's vendors. Therefore it is essential that Gap make their new standards and requirements clear, especially to vendors who have previously supplied Gap. The objectives of the relationship need to be agreed between the two parties. Gap may find it advisable to award prototype contracts to give vendors a feel for what it is like working with Gap in this new way.

[Paragraph 6]

Once selected any subsequent monitoring system of vendors should be used to reinforce not weaken the relationship and so should not just be a tool for criticism but also one that recognises improvement. It should be based on key agreed performance measures and used to provide feedback, encourage improvement and reinforce Gap's expectations. Any vendor struggling to achieve its targets should be encouraged to work with Gap through, for example, a vendor development or improvement group.

[Paragraph 7]

The information provided by the monitoring system must also be sufficient to enable decisions on sourcing for future products to be made. Although Gap and its vendors should develop joint long-term business strategies, they must recognise business partnerships are not necessarily for life. Environmental changes may mean that a previously rejected vendor becomes more suitable to the organisation's needs. Gap could also change what they require from their suppliers, for example they may look for companies who can design, develop and produce products and this would require vendors with different capabilities to those just selected for production.

[Paragraph 8]

Developing closer relationships with its suppliers could have significant benefits for Gap in securing its long-term future. Having vendors who can work alongside Gap's designers could reduce development lead times. The closer relationship with their supply base could also be used strategically by Gap, with the management team managing the whole process from vendor to customer as a fully integrated supply chain, in an attempt to reduce the late deliveries and inventory problems that Gap experienced in 2000.

(Source: OU Business School student assignment)

Extract 5.6

The process by which Toyota has arrived at its supplier list should be assimilated by any European supplier seeking a share of Japanese 'transplant' business, which is expected to continue expanding in Europe throughout the next decade. [...]

The selection process is already three years old. It began with Toyota's European administrative office in Brussels compiling initial data on 2,000 potential suppliers.

At this initial stage, 'we had open doors', recalls Jackson. 'Lots of companies came to talk to us off their own bat; some applied through contact with the SMMT (the UK's Society of Motor Manufacturers and Traders), some through chambers of commerce, and so on. There were too many to see individually so we checked their reputations, resources, customer bases, and so on, and there were some we could discard straight away.'

A little closer scrutiny left Toyota quickly able to whittle down the number in which it was seriously interested to 400 – already fewer than half the number of direct suppliers to most European vehicle makers.

Even this partial selection process serves to highlight one of the key differences between Japanese and European component supply structures. In the former, few but large 'first tier' suppliers account for more than 60 per cent of the total added-value of a vehicle, with thousands of small 'second tier' companies supplying the big component companies like Nippondenso. In Europe the number of direct suppliers is greater and they are more highly specialised.

'It's rather difficult to have a relationship with 1,000 suppliers,' observes Jackson. 'It's much better to have fewer, who are more closely involved.'

Closer involvement in Toyota's case has meant short-listed companies being asked to quote for entire product groups, not individual components, 'to give them a larger, more worthwhile chunk of the business,' says Jackson.

At the 400-candidate stage, the selection process became much more painstaking. Over a period of 10 months a number of multidisciplinary Toyota teams assessed capabilities according to four key criteria:

- management capability and attitude;
- production and manufacturing facilities, and level of investment in technology;
- quality control systems and philosophy;
- research and development capability.

This stage of weeding out reduced the 400 to 250, who were then asked to submit firm costs 'to give us a feel for price competition'. All were then deemed acceptable in terms of their potential to meet quality and price standards.

The first prototype parts orders were issued as far back as last October, and the stream of components is already flowing fast, with most expected to have been received by Toyota by the end of this month.

The awarding of prototype contracts means, if anything, an intensification of contacts between Toyota and its would-be production suppliers. Toyota is continuing to give a series of presentations to all of them to reinforce awareness of its expectations.

A total of eight such meetings have been held already, and another series will be held as the project moves from prototype stage to the awarding of production parts contracts. 'It's a physical demonstration that being a supplier to Toyota is going to be different,' stresses Jackson. 'You start to change your mind set. One of our philosophies is to motivate – people are capable of doing much more than is usually required of them, and we ask them to demonstrate it.'

(Source: *Financial Times*, 10 April 1991)

Extract 5.8

The process, Robinson claims, is a two-way street, with Toyota not necessarily seeking to impose Japanese methods by diktat. As one small example, Japanese and European manufacturers differ in the way gearshifts are usually made. But, says Robinson, it is clearly not cost-effective for a European factory to throw away large investments already made, 'so that supplier will be left to cope just as long as the product meets Toyota's standards'.

Suppliers have been left in no doubt what those standards are – they are showered with pro formas which minutely detail what has been discussed and understood between supplier and vehicle maker. For most suppliers, it was a wholly alien approach and many grumbled in the early stages that there was far too much paperwork. 'But then they came to realise that this way every eventuality gets covered. No-one has to interpret anything, because it's all there in black and white.'

'Subsequently', says Jackson, 'they have been very impressed by the thoroughness.' Toyota is, as yet, reticent about claiming that widespread attitude changes might be taking place – 'you can never be sure what goes on behind locked doors', says Jackson. 'But some have been very enthusiastic about making the investments needed, and they seem to expect that Toyota will make a lot of demands, particularly about quality. The ones that I've seen are all getting very much caught up in the process.'

The 1,850 unsuccessful would-be suppliers are being encouraged not to think they are permanently excluded. 'We've had a lot of replies to our "Dear John" letters at least thanking us for fairness and thoroughness of the selection process,' says Robinson. Adds Jackson: 'Those who failed have still got to be treated with respect. It is totally wrong for many of them to think we might have been saying they're not up to scratch – inherently within these organisations there is a lot of capability.'

Nor should they think they are excluded from Toyota business for good, he stresses. 'A widespread belief that Japanese vehicle companies form links for life with suppliers on a single-sourcing basing is wholly erroneous', he declares.

As for long-term relationships, they required continually to be earned, Jackson stresses. Throughout, Jackson emphasises Toyota's need for partnership with suppliers rather than the adversarial relationship between vehicle makers and their suppliers so common in Europe.

To that end, Toyota has set up technology 'help' teams. 'If a supplier has difficulty understanding what we want, or how to go about it, we really want to go out and explain our production systems to them. That might sound patronising but it's not intended to be … the idea really is to give assistance rather than check on what's been done.

At a personal level, Jackson and Robinson acknowledge some – not severe – culture shock. Within the European industry, says Jackson, he was used to instant decisions, involving little detail. 'It was 10 minutes to make the decision, 10 to implement it and three months to correct it. In Toyota there's three months' discussions, 10 minutes to approve it and no time correcting it.' There is, he says, a simple way to adjust – 'you just hang your ego on the coathook with your coat.'

(Source: *Financial Times*, 10 April 1991)

Extract 5.9

The supply chain and competitive performance

Traditionally most organisations have seen themselves as competing in order to survive. However, such a philosophy can be self-defeating if it leads to an unwillingness to co-operate. Behind this concept is the idea of supply chain integration.

The supply chain is the network of organisations that are involved in the different processes and activities that deliver products and services to the consumer. Thus for example a shirt manufacturer is a part of a supply chain that includes the weavers of fabrics, the manufacturers of fibres, distributors and retailers. Each of these organisations in the chain are dependent upon each other and yet do not closely co-operate with each other.

In the past it was often the case that relationships with suppliers, distributors or retailers were competitive rather than co-operative. It is still the case today that companies will seek to achieve cost reductions or profit improvement at the expense of their supply chain partners. Companies such as these do not realize that simply transferring costs to their suppliers or distributors does not make them any more competitive. The reason is that ultimately all costs will be reflected in the price paid by the end user. Leading companies recognise the fallacy of the conventional approach and instead seek to make the supply chain as a whole more competitive *overall*. They have realised that the real competition is not company against company but rather supply chain against supply chain.

(Source: based on Christopher, M., 2001, 'Logistics and competitive strategy', in Barnes, D., ed., *Understanding Business Processes*, London, Routledge/The Open University, Chapter 11, p. 157)

Text 5.10

Notwithstanding tales of great care taken in its vendor qualification process, Gap continues to attract criticism for working conditions in some of its suppliers. Outline the key aspects of a vendor selection and monitoring process that will further Gap's long-term best interests.

In many respects, Gap's long-term success depends upon its supply chain. However, as the case study points out, Gap clothing was produced in three thousand factories in over fifty countries in 2002.

For a multinational corporation such as Gap, the selection process is perhaps manageable but with so many factories to oversee, the monitoring process would require an army of vendor compliance officers. Reducing the number of suppliers that the company uses might overcome this problem but a better way would be to try to integrate external suppliers into the Gap 'system'. This sounds paradoxical but essentially it would mean Gap and its suppliers viewing the supply chain as a unitary system. Obviously, when one part of the system fails, it has adverse affects on other parts so it is in Gap's interest to integrate external vendors into its own system of production, distribution, standards and ethics. In this sense, the supply chain is not just about what Gap does but also about the way that it does it.

Gap's long-term success depends upon closer integration of its supply chain which can be achieved by establishing clear methods of communication. Inventory management through systems such as Enterprise Resource Planning for example are available to organisations like Gap and would help it to communicate its inventory requirements to suppliers. Integration must go further though to ensure that suppliers fully understand all of Gap's requirements, including production and ethical standards. Vendor compliance officers need to work closely with supplier management and reach understandings on which the supply chain is based. Toyota, for example, did this with its suppliers through clear written communication to ensure that there were no misunderstandings or ambiguities between parties. This may sound bureaucratic but given the potential for misinterpretation, especially taking into account the fact that Gap operates in a linguistically and culturally diverse global environment, this makes sense.

Gap understands that the monitoring and selection process is fundamental to the success of the business for two reasons. First, Gap operates in a highly competitive market. In this sense, the company knows that failure to manage its supply chain effectively leads to inefficiencies and the subsequent loss of competitive advantage resulting in inferior goods at higher prices. Second, the company is aware that its customers have a great deal of choice and will be looking or something beyond tangible functionality when buying their clothing. Maintaining moral standards of work throughout the supply chain is Gap's responsibility since it is Gap which sells the end product to discerning customers who ultimately make purchasing choices. Consumers now consume products to express their identity as much as because they need them. So maintaining ethical standards is of prime importance.

(Source: OU Business School student assignment)

Text 5.11

Notwithstanding tales of great care taken in its vendor qualification process, Gap continues to attract criticism for working conditions in some of its suppliers. Outline the key aspects of a vendor selection and monitoring process that will further Gap's long-term best interests.

The 1992 newspaper article by the Guardian accused Gap of employing Chinese labourers at less than $2 an hour for working 80 hours per week. This tarnished Gap's image and they put in place a code which was designed to eliminate this sort of thing happening again. Gap introduced Vendor Compliance Officers (VCOs) to encourage improvements and where necessary to terminate or suspend the vendors. They did this by on site visits, investigations of reported breaches and enforcing health and safety issues. This resulted in the termination of 120 vendors. (Minding the Gap 2004:13).

However, this did not stop criticism from the African Forum and Unite for what they saw as 'abusive working conditions' (Minding the Gap 2004:13). Gap needs a proper system of selection for its vendors in order to eliminate this sort of criticism. It has to decide what it wants from its vendors and how it is going to get the right vendors to apply.

What does Gap require from its vendors? Is it just a question of how quickly and cheaply they can produce Gap's products? It is true that if the clothes are not at the right price then they will not sell. So this is an important factor in awarding contracts and it could influence Gap when they select vendors. However, price is not the only consideration.

In an ideal world, Gap require vendors who have a strong management in terms of capability and attitude who are able to meet targets and cost and also maintain a happy workforce; proper production and manufacturing facilities; a level of investment that ensures continuing development of factory facilities and keeps costs down; and a quality control system.

How can Gap achieve this? They could invite prospective vendors to visit Gap to see if they meet the requirements stated above. It is possible that over half these organisations will not meet this first set of standards. They could then set prototype tasks, to see how potential vendors perform. Following on from this there would need to be many meetings and interviews in order to select the right organisations for a long-term working partnership that is stable and workable.

These interviews and discussions take time to get right. There can be no short cuts if Gap wants to eliminate the sort of criticism it has been receiving. With the pressures of quality, demand, price, and shareholders' demand for a return on their money, there is a risk that short cuts will be taken and the rigorous interviews and checks may not be carried out. Bryan Jackson UK Director (Toyota) describes this way of working: 'It was 10 minutes to make the decision, 10 to implement and three months to correct it'. The Toyota way is that it is better to have 'Three months discussions, 10 minutes to approve it and no time correcting it.' (Source: *Financial Times*, 10 April 1991). If Gap took on board this Toyota way it would ensure less criticism in future.

(Source: OU Business School student assignment)

Text 5.12

Nike and the vexed issue of corporate responsibility

In the early 1990s, as the first factories in Indonesia were opened, the leading training shoe companies' strategy of using low-cost Asian labour to manufacture their products came under increasing scrutiny from human rights groups, Christian organisations and even academic institutions. By the end of the decade, campaign groups aimed at stamping out this so-called 'sweatshop' production were active in the USA, the UK and Australia. Media interest in the topic was widespread, to the extent that UK magazine *The Big Issue* was urging its readers not to buy Nike trainers and US satirist Garry Trudeau featured the subject in an 11-part *Doonesbury* cartoon series.

Most criticism was aimed at the major trainer manufacturers, especially Nike, for reasons of their size and market dominance. The emphasis Nike and its competitors placed on social betterment through physical fitness in their advertising also made them more vulnerable to accusations of mistreatment of their Asian workers. Initially, the trainer companies tried to divert criticism by claiming that the issue was the responsibility of their subcontractors, but were soon forced to respond when the subject was drawn to the attention of the US State Department. Eventually they were obliged to draw up codes of conduct in an attempt to eradicate human rights abuses in their factories, raise wages, ban harmful chemicals and eradicate the use of under-age labour. This was not sufficient for their critics; instead, it proved to be the first stage in a cycle of criticism and reaction which is still continuing, with the focus shifting from Indonesia to China and Vietnam, and manufacturers still struggling to establish a socially 'responsible' image.

While criticism of human rights abuses in training shoe factories is clearly justified, it is interesting to examine the trainer manufacturers' operations in the context of the prevailing economic situation in countries such as Vietnam and China. Their presence in these countries can be economically critical. China is now the biggest shoe producing country in the world; Nike is Vietnam's biggest employer. Jobs are scarce and people want to work for companies like Nike and Reebok. Factory jobs, while badly paid by Western standards, pay twice as much as teachers earn in Vietnam.

Nevertheless, as a result of the continued criticism, corporate responsibility is now a major concern for all trainer companies whose shoes are manufactured in Southeast Asia and China. In 1998 Nike appointed its first new vice-president for corporate and social responsibility and introduced six new corporate responsibility initiatives:

1   *Working conditions* – The company guaranteed to expedite the changeover from use of solvent-based chemicals to use of water-based substitutes in its factories.

2   *Age limits* – The minimum age limit for factory workers was raised to 18 in all footwear manufacturing and 16 in other types of manufacturing (clothing and accessories). Footwear factory managers were obliged to guarantee not to employ anyone under this age.

3   *Independent monitoring* – Nike pledged to secure independent monitoring of conditions in its factories by involving non-governmental organisations (aid agencies) in the process.

4   *Education* – The company announced plans to expand in-factory education programmes in all Nike footwear factories.

5   *Small business finance* – Support for a microfinance loan programme aimed at stimulating the establishment of small businesses in Vietnam, Indonesia, Pakistan and Thailand was increased.

6   *Research funding* – Nike pledged to provide funding for research 'to explore issues related to global manufacturing and responsible business practices' such as independent monitoring and health issues.

[...]

For trainer manufacturers, taking the issue of corporate responsibility seriously is not just a response to continued criticism, but is also perceived as an important means of establishing their credibility with their consumers, current and future, as they attempt to expand sales of their products throughout the world.

(Source: adapted from Sturges, J., 2000, Case Study, 'Keep on running: the training shoe business', pp. 24, 26–27, The Open University Business School)

Session 6 resources

Text 6.1

Paragraph number	Essay text	Notes on structure
[P1]	**Compare and contrast Gap's staff management with its outsourcing policy.**	
[P2]	**Introduction**	
[P3]	Gap chooses to manage its staff in the way that it does for the same reason that it chooses to outsource its manufacturing. That is, the company seeks to optimise overall performance of Gap Inc. This analysis will compare the two policies starting with an overview of outsourcing.	Very high-level paragraph Introduces the two key concepts from the title Connects them by a similarity Points forward to how analysis will be structured
[P4]	**Outsourcing**	Subheading frames section with first main concept
[P5]	In Gap's case, outsourcing refers to the externalisation of its production processes. Gap chooses the open market for the manufacturing of its garments as opposed to producing them internally because of the benefits that the open market provides. Labour markets in foreign countries provide cheaper sources of the routine labour required in the manufacturing process than Gap can find in its home markets. Effective management of the supply chain can lead to competitive advantage through cost reduction (labour and materials), output flexibility (quantity and type) and economies of scale developed through task specialisation of each of its suppliers (Mabey et al., 2000, p. 177). Outsourcing also allows Gap to focus on its core processes. These include designing clothes, marketing, distribution and sales. Gap does not create value during the manufacturing process. Just as Nike does not consider itself as a manufacturer of sports shoes, Gap is not a manufacturer of leisure clothing.	Defines concept and then moves down to a lower level of details Explains reason Explains further (lower level details) Explains further using several key business concepts Refers to business studies course material Explains further using another key concept, *core processes* Gives details to explain concept Conclusion of section moves up to high level generalisation and refers to another case study

[P6]

Management of employees: core versus periphery

[P7]

Because outsourcing involves the crossing of organisational boundaries, Gap does not have to concern itself too deeply with the human resource management implications for non-Gap employees working in the manufacturing process, which as I have already suggested, is a peripheral process. Peripheral employees like these are likely to be unskilled, poorly paid and carry out menial, repetitive tasks. This situation can be contrasted with Gap's own employees who enjoy excellent working conditions and receive an array of benefits above and beyond pay and holiday. For example, they have good career prospects, access to a heath and well being programme and may receive financial assistance for things like moving house, travel and study. The reason for the difference is that Gap's own workers are involved in core processes. They can therefore be labelled as 'core' workers and are viewed as an essential resource of the company. The market for employees who possess 'core' skills is fiercely competitive so Gap must seek to establish a human resources approach geared at attracting, retaining and motivating its employees.

[P8]

One facet of an HRM approach to staff management is the concept of corporate culture which can loosely be defined as a set of shared values and beliefs aimed at promoting greater levels of enthusiasm and commitment within the organisation. In this regard, Gap's staff management can be seen as a vehicle for achievement and is designed to have a positive psychological impact on human inputs to extract a greater quality of output. Outsourcing on the other hand enables Gap to focus on its core processes and reduce costs. This implies that Gap neither has the knowledge or capital to invest in workers involved in the manufacturing process. As such, it must allow its suppliers to determine their own human resource strategies as long as they

---

Subheading frames section with second main concept, *staff management* and introduces new key concept *corporate culture*

High-level generalisation about human resource management of periphery makes link back to previous section

Explains generalisation

Gives details

Frames contrast using *core versus periphery* concept

Generalises about core working conditions

Moves down to low-level examples to explain

Explains similarity

Gives further details

Introduces new concept *corporate culture* to frame contrast

Defines concept

Uses concept to explain *management policy*

Uses cause-effect to explain

Moves back to *corporate culture* concept. Uses cause-effect to explain

Gives details to show contrast

are in keeping with Gap's own strategic vision and conform to Gap's principles. Besides, in general, the nature of work in the manufacturing process requires little creativity. It can be regarded as automated, impersonal, and in many respects bureaucratic. Employers do not need to win the hearts and minds of its employees — the fact that there are few alternative places to work combined with the number of people who live in poverty is motivation enough to work hard.

Uses cause–effect to explain

[P9]
Market demand and job (in)security

Subheading introduces four new concepts

[P10]
Surprisingly, Gap's staff management and its outsourcing policy do share some similar ground. The job security of both sets of employees is to a large extent determined by market forces. A downturn in demand for example might lead Gap to reduce both its domestic workforce (case study p. 15) as well as output (case study p. 12). Furthermore, both staff management and Gap's outsourcing policy play a role in determining those levels of demand. Internally for example, marketing, design and sales can help with the qualitative aspects of demand while the efficient production processes can bring down costs.

First sentence signals *similarity*

Generalisation frames similarity with key concept of *market forces*

Explains how concept works with low-level example

Refers to case study

Explains similarity further

Explains with another low-level example

[P11]
Conclusion

Summarises how analysis was done

[P12]
The concept of outsourcing was elucidated and reasons given to explain why Gap chooses to outsource. It was then argued that there exists a stark contrast in the nature of work, conditions and benefits received across the organisation's boundary using the concept of corporate culture to highlight these differences between them. Finally, it was suggested both outsourcing and internal staff management are both subject to market forces.

Repeats explanation of concept *outsourcing* at very high level of generalisation

Repeats explanation of contrast analysis framed by concept *outsourcing*

Repeats explanation of similarity analysis framed by concept *market forces*

(Source: OU Business School student assignment)

Extract 6.2

Introduction

Wal-Mart's active and ambitious takeover strategy has removed constraints that would otherwise limit its expansion; one of Wal-Mart's major UK competitors has been eliminated as a result of the Asda takeover (Costello, 1995, p.86). Although initial investment was costly (£6.7billion according to Wal-Mart's Annual Report, 2000), and not without risk, large benefits for Wal-Mart have followed, especially in comparison to investment in other countries:

> "It took Wal-Mart International five years to invade Europe. When it did, making three acquisitions in two years, one foot landed in quicksand, in Germany. The other touched a gold mine, in Britain" (Levine, 2004, p.80).

This is evidenced by "expanding sales from $16.8 billion in 1999 to $21.7billion [in 2003]" (Levine, 2004, p.80) and market share increase, sales and retail space growth as explained in the case study (Asda–Wal-Mart case study, p.4), culminating in Wal-Mart becoming the "largest company and the biggest employer in the world" (p.2).

Expansion

Wal-Mart's UK success arises from several factors in its Asda takeover. Expansion allows for broader activities to be carried out within the organisation (Costello, 1995, p.85–86). As more activities are brought in-house, costs usually decrease and control increases over confidentiality, availability and co-ordination. Sloman & Sutcliffe, however, argue that co-ordination becomes complex and diseconomies of scale can arise because "lines of communication become longer and more complex" (1998, p.204). They also suggest that language is costly to a company moving into a foreign market (p.203) but in the Asda–Wal-Mart case, the common language has proved a benefit to both companies in comparison to problems experienced in Germany (Asda–Wal-Mart case study, p.6).

Although the issues surrounding language have been irrelevant to the Asda takeover, Sloman & Sutcliffe (1998, p.204) do point to the perceived imposition of foreign strategies causing hostility, particularly with US multinational corporations (MNCs). Whysall highlights the points of contrast between Wal-Mart and Asda:

> "Wal-Mart is used to operating from significantly larger outlets from the typical Asda ... Wal-Mart's expertise lies in selling a wide range of general merchandise" (Whysall, 2001, p.731)

However, he also explains that the stores are of similar types in that they are both "larger than competitors' stores; they operate on low profit margins; and they offer a wide selection of discounted merchandise" (2001, p.733). The case study reflects this latter point, stating that, "there was always going to be a good fit between Asda and Wal-Mart" (Asda–Wal-Mart case study, p.4), as both companies operate similar marketing and price strategies.

(Source: OU Business School student assignment)

Text 6.3

Compare and contrast Gap's staff management with its outsourcing policy.

Gap's management of its employment process [1]_____ _____ related to the strategic importance placed on its different business functions.

Gap has recognised that the manufacturing process does not make its product 'unique'. Consequently, it does not own any of the factories that make its goods. Instead, Gap's management has made the decision to 'outsource', i.e. sub-contract production to external, independent companies world-wide. This gives Gap a [4]_____, it:

- Avoids investment in manufacturing infrastructure
- Results in lower manufacturing costs by sourcing from low-cost producers
- Enables poor quality products to be rejected
- Gives increased flexibility of supply which can be increased or reduced according to demand

In human resource management terms, outsourcing [5]_____ _____ a 'hard' approach focusing on cost reductions and efficiencies. By contrast, Gap's style of management of its own staff, those involved in its core activities (design, marketing, distribution and retail) [7]_____the 'soft' side of human resource management which "stresses the importance of empowering staff, of ensuring their commitment, of releasing their creativity and energy" (Study Guide 4, p. 27) as Gap themselves acknowledge, "It takes thousands of passionate, dedicated and talented employees to deliver the merchandise and shopping experience our customers expect and deserve' (Minding the Gap, p. 11).

Gap [8]_____ bought into the message of supporters of 'corporate culture'. Gaining the support and commitment of employees, giving them a "sense of belonging ... a sense of excitement in the job" (Thompson and McHugh, p. 142) [9]_____ an organisation's performance.

Gap considers it sufficiently important that employees can relate to the company's values and goals that it has introduced a rewards and recognition programme where employees are acknowledged not only for their individual performance, but also for their support of company goals with President's awards being given to outstanding employees (Minding the Gap, p. 11), all backed up by [11]_____ including health care, family support, personal development and career planning and financial assistance.

Its support for those who do volunteer work in the community and donations through Gap Foundation to charitable organisations also help to promote the feeling that Gap is [12]_____

_____.

13 _____ that Gap's policies favour their core staff to the detriment of workers in the manufacturing plants as both groups of employees are protected by clearly documented employment policies.

Despite the fact that Gap does not directly employ the workers in the manufacturing facilities, they do acknowledge some responsibility for them. They have responded to criticisms that the workers in their factories are being exploited through the introduction of the Code of Vendor Conduct in 1992. It aimed to influence working conditions and management practices, including the right to join labour unions, with account taken of cultural differences. 15_____ _____ the code is not voluntary. In 2002 Gap terminated business with a number of vendors who were in breach of it. Gap has also introduced a Global Compliance Team that is responsible for monitoring overseas vendors, making site visits, investigating alleged reports of breaches of the Code, enforcing corrective actions in areas of health and safety, etc.

16 _____.

With Gap having 3,000 factories spread over 50 countries
17 _____all non-conformances can be investigated or even reported. Workers employed in these factories
18 _____ well paid and lucky to have regular employment and so unwilling to report any non-compliance. On the contrary, 20_____ aware the Code exists.
21 _____ _____ without the support of external pressure groups employees' rights are still being undermined. As recently as 2002 Gap was criticised for "abusive working conditions" — a combination of long hours, low pay, health hazards and exploitative management practices (Minding the Gap, p. 13) in at least six countries.

Gap has 22_____ for its own staff, backing up "its philosophy of diversity and equal opportunity with a policy of zero tolerance for discriminatory behaviour on any grounds" (Minding the Gap, p. 12) 23_____ _____in the field of equal opportunities.

Gap staff management and its outsourcing policy
24 _____ _____
25 _____. Although all staff are protected by company policies, significant
26 _____. The conditions of employment of core staff (management, designers, etc.) are 27_____ _____ On the other hand, peripheral, manufacturing workers are often still subject to
28 _____

to Gap re-sourcing production to alternative locations based on commercial considerations.

(Source: OU Business School student assignment)

Appendix: Simplified texts

Extract 5.1

Simplified version of Extract E

The first two paragraphs of Miriam's assignment (Extract E) and the simplified version

Original text	Simplified text
Gap continues to attract criticism for working conditions in some of its suppliers. Outline the key aspects of a vendor selection and monitoring process that will further Gap's long-term best interests.	**Gap continues to be criticised for the working conditions in some of its suppliers. Outline a process for selecting suppliers (or vendors) and monitoring supplier's performance which will help Gap.**
Gap's current vendor selection policy focuses on a vendor's ability to meet product quality standards and production capacity at the right cost, and also on whether they conform to ethical trading standards in line with the Code of Vendor Conduct.	Gap has a vendor selection policy which focuses on two things about a vendor. First, are they able to supply good quality products and are they able to deliver products at the right cost? Second, do they meet Gap's ethical trading standards? These standards are outlined in the Code of Vendor Conduct.
However, this policy has not stopped criticism of the working practices of some of Gap's suppliers. It may therefore be beneficial for Gap to consider recent trends in vendor selection whereby organisations seek close long-term relationships with suppliers. These relationships are called 'partnership sourcing' and are considered mutually beneficial to both parties.	However, this policy has not stopped criticism of the working practices of some of Gap's suppliers. It may therefore be beneficial for Gap to consider recent trends in vendor selection whereby organisations seek close long-term relationships with suppliers. These relationships are called 'partnership sourcing' and are considered mutually beneficial to both parties.

(Source: OU Business School student assignment)

Extract 5.3

Simplified version of Extract 5.2

Original text	Simplified text
Supplier selection and partnership sourcing	Supplier selection and partnership sourcing
[Paragraph 1]	**[Paragraph 1]**
Supplier selection is becoming a much more important aspect of the purchasing process for many organisations. Recent trends in purchasing have seen many organisations seeking to have much closer, long-term relationships with many fewer suppliers. The term partnership sourcing has come into currency, and is in many respects similar to relationship marketing. With whom to have that relationship has become a vitally important decision.	For many organisations, supplier selection is becoming a much more important aspect of the process of purchasing supplies. More and more organisations are trying to have closer, long-term relationships with fewer suppliers. The term 'partnership sourcing' is used to describe this process. In many respects, it is similar to relationship marketing. In both, it is vitally important to choose the right organisation to have a relationship with.
[Paragraph 2]	**[Paragraph 2]**
The following article from the Financial Times explains how Toyota selects its suppliers. It was written at the time when motor manufacturing giant Toyota was setting up a production facility in Europe for the first time. It provides a fascinating insight into Japanese approaches to purchasing. Note the emphasis that Toyota place on selecting their suppliers, and the huge amount of work that they put into the selection process.	The following article from the Financial Times explains how Toyota selects its suppliers. It was written at the time when motor manufacturing giant Toyota was setting up a production facility in Europe for the first time. It provides a fascinating insight into Japanese approaches to purchasing. Note the emphasis that Toyota place on selecting their suppliers, and the huge amount of work that they put into the selection process.
HOW TOYOTA FILTERS ITS COMPONENT SUPPLIERS	**HOW TOYOTA CHOOSES SUPPLIERS OF ITS CAR-PARTS**
[Paragraph 3]	**[Paragraph 3]**
Toyota, Japan's largest car maker, is in the very last stages of whittling down to 150, from 2,000, the would-be suppliers of prototype components to its £700m UK car plant now under construction in Derbyshire.	Toyota is Japan's largest car maker. It is building a car plant in Derbyshire for £700m. It is choosing companies who can supply the kinds of car parts it needs. It has nearly finished choosing. It has reduced the list of suppliers from 2000 to 150.
[Paragraph 4]	**[Paragraph 4]**
Toyota would be desperately vulnerable to any shortcomings in its parts suppliers. It buys in 75 per cent of the value of its cars, compared with only around one half for European vehicle makers.	Toyota would have great difficulties if any of its suppliers were not reliable. This is because the parts it buys from suppliers are worth 75% of the value of the car. This is less than European car manufacturers. They buy parts worth 50% of the value of the car from suppliers.

[Paragraph 5]

Yet far from 'importing' tried-and-trusted Japanese suppliers, Toyota insists that when all its Derby suppliers are disclosed they will include only a handful of Japanese companies. The vast majority, it says, will be based in the UK and continental Europe.

[Paragraph 6]

Toyota is paying more than lip service to maximising 'local' (EC, not just UK) content, insists Bryan Jackson, a Toyota Motor Manufacturing UK director, and Jim Robinson, its parts procurement manager who has overseen the selection process.

[Paragraph 7]

The point was underlined by managing director Yukihisa Hirano at a Welsh Development Agency conference last month when he talked of 'mis-perceptions' about the so-called Japanese 'transplants'.

[Paragraph 8]

'Toyota has never asked any Japanese companies to set up in Europe', Hirano declared. 'Among the companies from whom we have ordered prototype parts only a few are Japanese, and they were established in Europe before we made our decision to manufacture here.'

[Paragraph 9]

The list has been drawn up on the basis that the companies' technological abilities, investments in research and development, plant, equipment and other resources are of a standard that should allow long-term partnerships to develop with Toyota.

[Paragraph 5]

However, Toyota are not bringing Japanese suppliers to Europe. They will use only a few Japanese companies. Most of their suppliers will be from the UK and Europe.

[Paragraph 6]

Toyota is not just saying it will use local suppliers from the UK and Europe. It really will use them. This is the view of Bryan Jackson, who is a Toyota Manufacturing UK director, and Jim Robinson, who is a 'parts procurement manager' (someone who organises the purchasing of car parts). Robinson has been responsible for the process of selecting the car-parts suppliers.

[Paragraph 7]

This view is supported by Toyota managing director, Yukihisa Hirano. He was speaking at a Welsh Development Agency conference last month. He said it was not true (a 'misperception') that Japanese companies in Europe bring other Japanese companies ('transplants') into Europe to supply them.

[Paragraph 8]

'Toyota has never asked any Japanese companies to set up in Europe,' Hirano said. 'Among the companies from whom we have ordered prototype parts only a few are Japanese, and they were established in Europe before we made our decision to manufacture here.'

[Paragraph 9]

The suppliers that have been chosen for the list are the suppliers that look like they will be able to have a long-term partnership with Toyota. They have been chosen on the basis of their technological abilities, investments in research and development, and plant, equipment and other resources.

Extract 5.5

Simplified version of Text 5.4, Miriam's completed assignment

Original text	Simplified text
Gap continues to attract criticism for working conditions in some of its suppliers. Outline the key aspects of a vendor selection and monitoring process that will further Gap's long-term best interests.	Gap continues to be criticised for the working conditions in some of its suppliers. Outline a process for selecting suppliers (or vendors) and monitoring suppliers' performance which will help Gap.
[Paragraph 1]	**[Paragraph 1]**
Gap's current vendor selection policy focuses on a vendor's ability to meet product quality standards and production capacity at the right cost and also on whether they conform to ethical trading standards in line with the Code of Vendor Conduct.	Gap has a vendor selection policy which focuses on two things about a vendor. First, are they able to supply good quality products and are they able to deliver products at the right cost? Second, do they meet Gap's ethical trading standards? These standards are outlined in the Code of Vendor Conduct.
[Paragraph 2]	**[Paragraph 2]**
However this policy has not stopped criticism of the working practices of some of Gap's suppliers. It may therefore be beneficial for Gap to consider recent trends in vendor selection whereby organisations seek close long-term relationships with suppliers. These relationships are called 'partnership sourcing' and are considered mutually beneficial to both parties.	However, this policy has not stopped criticism of the working practices of some of Gap's suppliers. It may therefore be beneficial for Gap to consider recent trends in vendor selection whereby organisations seek close long-term relationships with suppliers. These relationships are called 'partnership sourcing', and are considered mutually beneficial to both parties.
[Paragraph 3]	**[Paragraph 3]**
If Gap was interested in partnership sourcing it would have to significantly reduce the number of vendors it deals with. As Bryan Jackson, director of Toyota Motor Manufacturing UK points out 'It's rather difficult to have a relationship with 1,000 suppliers ... It's much better to have fewer, who are more closely involved' (OU-B200, Study Guide 3, p. 38).	If Gap wanted to use partnership sourcing, it would have to deal with fewer vendors. As Bryan Jackson, director of Toyota Motor Manufacturing UK points out 'It's rather difficult to have a relationship with 1,000 suppliers ... It's much better to have fewer, who are more closely involved' (OU Study Guide 3, p. 38).
[Paragraph 4]	**[Paragraph 4]**
Vendors could be selected to provide a larger share of the organisation's business, supplying whole product groups (one vendor for jeans; one for T-shirts, etc). What Gap should be looking for in these suppliers is more than just their ability to deliver the product. It should also look for an understanding of company philosophy,	Vendors could be selected to provide a larger share of the organisation's business. For example, they could supply whole product groups (one vendor for jeans; one vendor for T-shirts, etc.). Gap should look at more than whether a supplier can deliver a product. Gap should look at the company's philosophy, management ability

management capability and attitude, and development capability. These are the items which the Toyota selection system, for example, pays significant attention to.

[Paragraph 5]

This form of customer-supplier relationship is obviously different to that previously experienced by Gap's vendors. Therefore it is essential that Gap make their new standards and requirements clear, especially to vendors who have previously supplied Gap. The objectives of the relationship need to be agreed between the two parties. Gap may find it advisable to award prototype contracts to give vendors a feel for what it is like working with Gap in this new way.

[Paragraph 6]

Once selected any subsequent monitoring system of vendors should be used to reinforce not weaken the relationship and so should not just be a tool for criticism but also one that recognises improvement. It should be based on key agreed performance measures and used to provide feedback, encourage improvement and reinforce Gap's expectations. Any vendor struggling to achieve its targets should be encouraged to work with Gap through, for example, a vendor development or improvement group.

[Paragraph 7]

The information provided by the monitoring system must also be sufficient to enable decisions on sourcing for future products to be made. Although Gap and its vendors should develop joint long-term business strategies, they must recognise business partnerships are not necessarily for life. Environmental changes may mean that a previously rejected vendor becomes more suitable to the organisation's needs. Gap could also change what they require from their suppliers, for example they may look for companies who can design, develop and produce products and this would require vendors with different capabilities to those just selected for production.

and attitude, and ability to develop new products. These are the items which the Toyota selection system, for example, pays special attention to.

[Paragraph 5]

This form of customer–supplier relationship is obviously different from what Gap's vendors are used to. Therefore, it is essential that Gap make their new standards and requirements clear, especially to vendors who have previously supplied Gap. The objectives of the relationship need to be agreed between the two parties. Gap may find it advisable to award practice contracts to give vendors a feel for what it is like working with Gap in this new way.

[Paragraph 6]

Once a vendor has been selected, the vendor monitoring process should be used to build the relationship. It should not be used to criticise the vendor and weaken the relationship. It should recognise improvement in the vendor. It should be based on key agreed performance measures and be used to provide feedback, encourage improvement and reinforce Gap's expectations. Any vendor that is struggling to achieve its targets should be encouraged to work with Gap through, for example, a vendor development or improvement group.

[Paragraph 7]

There must be enough information from the monitoring system so that Gap and the vendors can make decisions about sourcing new products in the future. Gap and its vendors should develop joint long-term business strategies, but they must recognise business partnerships are not necessarily for life. Environmental changes may mean that a vendor who was previously rejected becomes more suitable to the organisation's needs. Gap could also change what they require from their suppliers. For example, they may look for companies who can design and develop products as well as produce them. They would require vendors with different capabilities to those vendors who were selected only for production.

[Paragraph 8]

Developing closer relationships with its suppliers could have significant benefits for Gap in securing its long-term future. Having vendors who can work alongside Gap's designers could reduce development lead times. The closer relationship with their supply base could also be used strategically by Gap, with the management team managing the whole process from vendor to customer as a fully integrated supply chain, in an attempt to reduce the late deliveries and inventory problems that Gap experienced in 2000.

[Paragraph 8]

If Gap develops closer relationships with its suppliers, this could have significant benefits for Gap. It could make its long-term future secure. If Gap had vendors who could work together with Gap's designers, this could reduce the time it takes to develop products. The closer relationship with the suppliers could also be used strategically by Gap. The management team could manage the whole process from vendor to customer as a fully integrated supply chain. This could reduce the late deliveries and inventory problems that Gap had in 2000.

Extract 5.7

Simplified version of Extract 5.6

Original text	Simplified text
The process by which Toyota has arrived at its supplier list should be assimilated by any European supplier seeking a share of Japanese 'transplant' business, which is expected to continue expanding in Europe throughout the next decade.	The process Toyota used to produce its list of suppliers should be used by any European supplier who wants to be a part of Japanese business coming to Europe. This is expected to continue expanding in Europe for the next 10 years.
The selection process is already three years old. It began with Toyota's European administrative office in Brussels compiling initial data on 2,000 potential suppliers.	The selection process began three years ago. First, Toyota's European administrative office in Brussels gathered information on 2,000 possible suppliers.
At this initial stage, 'we had open doors', recalls Jackson. 'Lots of companies came to talk to us off their own bat; some applied through contact with the SMMT (the UK's Society of Motor Manufacturers and Traders), some through chambers of commerce, and so on. There were too many to see individually so we checked their reputations, resources, customer bases, and so on, and there were some we could discard straight away.'	At this early stage, 'we had open doors', recalls Jackson. 'Lots of companies came to talk to us off their own bat; some applied through contact with the SMMT (the UK's Society of Motor Manufacturers and Traders), some through chambers of commerce, and so on. There were too many to see individually so we checked their reputations, resources, customer bases, and so on, and there were some we could discard straight away.'
A little closer scrutiny left Toyota quickly able to whittle down the number in which it was seriously interested to 400 – already fewer than half the number of direct suppliers to most European vehicle makers.	After more investigation, Toyota could reduce the number of serious suppliers to 400. This was already fewer than half of the number of direct suppliers to most European vehicle makers

Even this partial selection process serves to highlight one of the key differences between Japanese and European component supply structures. In the former, few but large 'first tier' suppliers account for more than 60 per cent of the total added-value of a vehicle, with thousands of small 'second tier' companies supplying the big component companies like Nippondenso. In Europe the number of direct suppliers is greater and they are more highly specialised.

'It's rather difficult to have a relationship with 1,000 suppliers,' observes Jackson. 'It's much better to have fewer, who are more closely involved.'

Closer involvement in Toyota's case has meant short-listed companies being asked to quote for entire product groups, not individual components, 'to give them a larger, more worthwhile chunk of the business,' says Jackson.

At the 400-candidate stage, the selection process became much more painstaking. Over a period of 10 months a number of multidisciplinary Toyota teams assessed capabilities according to four key criteria:

- management capability and attitude;
- production and manufacturing facilities, and level of investment in technology;
- quality control systems and philosophy;
- research and development capability.

This stage of weeding out reduced the 400 to 250, who were then asked to submit firm costs 'to give us a feel for price competition'. All were then deemed acceptable in terms of their potential to meet quality and price standards.

This is only the first part of the selection process. But it already shows one of the key differences between Japanese and European car-parts supply chains. In Japanese supply chains, suppliers known as 'first tier' suppliers supply more than 60% of the total added value of a car. There are also thousands of smaller 'second tier' companies which supply the first tier suppliers, for example, Nippondenso. In European supply chains there are many more direct suppliers. These European direct suppliers are more highly specialised than Japanese ones.

'It's rather difficult to have a relationship with 1,000 suppliers,' observes Jackson. 'It's much better to have fewer, who are more closely involved.'

Because companies are more closely involved with Toyota, they are asked to supply entire product groups, not separate vehicle parts. This is 'to give them a larger, more worthwhile chunk of the business,' says Jackson.

When Toyota had reduced the number of suppliers to 400, they became much more careful with the selection process. Over a period of 10 months, a number of Toyota teams made up of specialists from different departments judged the suppliers. They used four key criteria:

- management capability and attitude
- production and manufacturing facilities, and level of investment in technology
- quality control systems and philosophy
- research and development capability.

This stage of the selection process cut the numbers of suppliers from 400 to 250. These were asked to tell Toyota how much it would cost to get supplies from them. This was 'to give us a feel for price competition'. All were judged to be acceptable on the basis of their ability to meet Toyota's standards on quality and price.

The first prototype parts orders were issued as far back as last October, and the stream of components is already flowing fast, with most expected to have been received by Toyota by the end of this month.

The awarding of prototype contracts means, if anything, an intensification of contacts between Toyota and its would-be production suppliers. Toyota is continuing to give a series of presentations to all of them to reinforce awareness of its expectations.

A total of eight such meetings have been held already, and another series will be held as the project moves from prototype stage to the awarding of production parts contracts. 'It's a physical demonstration that being a supplier to Toyota is going to be different,' stresses Jackson. 'You start to change your mind set. One of our philosophies is to motivate – people are capable of doing much more than is usually required of them, and we ask them to demonstrate it.'

Toyota issued the first sample orders as long ago as last October. The components are already being supplied to Toyota at a fast rate. Most of them will arrive before the end of this month.

When these sample contracts are given to suppliers, there is even more contact between Toyota and the suppliers who want to work for Toyota. Toyota continues to give a series of presentations to the suppliers to keep on reminding them of what Toyota expects from them.

There have already been eight meetings like this. There will be another series of meetings as the project moves from this prototype stage to the stage where the real contracts for components are set up. 'It's a physical demonstration that being a supplier to Toyota is going to be different,' stresses Jackson. 'You start to change your mind set. One of our philosophies is to motivate – people are capable of doing much more than is usually required of them, and we ask them to demonstrate it.'

(Source: *Financial Times*, 10 April 1991)

Acknowledgements

Grateful acknowledgement is made to the following sources:

Text

Extract 1.3, Text 1.18: Finch, J. (1999) 'AA set for a float vote', *Guardian Unlimited* © Guardian Newspapers Limited 2006; Extracts 1.4, 1.15, 1.16, Text 1.11, 1.17: Taylor, P. (2003), 'US airlines: Big carriers unlikely to find much relief' by Paul Taylor, *Financial Times*, 30 January 2003. Copyright © Financial Times. Reproduced by permission; Extracts 1.7, 1.8, 2.1, Text 2.9, 2.13, 2.14, 2.15, 2.16: Capon, C. (2004) *Understanding Organisational Context*, Prentice-Hall, 2nd edition, Pearson Education Limited © Pearson Education Limited, 2000, 2004. Reproduced by permission; Text 3.4: *The Toronto Star*, 8 August 2006, © 2006 Bloomberg L.P. All rights reserved. Reprinted with permission; Text 4.1: Houlder, V. (1997) 'Alternative to poaching: how companies can collaborate to beat skills shortages', *Financial Times*, 13 February 1997, Copyright © 1997, Financial Times. Reproduced by permission; Text 4.2: Based on Teather, D. (2002) 'Finance: It's a game of more bubble for your bucks: Coca-Cola tries to find a new flavour as Pepsi stays on the ball, stealing US market', *The Guardian*, 2 April 2002. Copyright © Guardian News & Media Ltd 1999. Reproduced by permission; Text 4.5: Adapted from Mathiason, N. (2007) Business & Media Business: 'Gap's next sale could be its last ....', *The Observer*, 14 January 2007 and Clark, A. (2007) 'Plenty of Gaps on the high street ...', *The Guardian*, 13 January 2007; Extracts 5.2 (insert), 5.6, 5.7, 5.8: 'How Toyota filters it component suppliers', *Financial Times*, 10 April 1991.